Introduction to Working with Manuscripts for Medievalists

Gorgias Handbooks

Gorgias Handbooks provides students and scholars with reference books, textbooks and introductions to different topics or fields of study. In this series, Gorgias welcomes books that are able to communicate information, ideas and concepts effectively and concisely, with useful reference bibliographies for further study.

Introduction to
Working with Manuscripts
for Medievalists

János M. Bak

2017

Gorgias Press LLC, 954 River Road, Piscataway, NJ, 08854, USA

www.gorgiaspress.com

Copyright © 2017 by Gorgias Press LLC

All rights reserved under International and Pan-American Copyright Conventions. No part of this publication may be reproduced, stored in a retrieval system or transmitted in any form or by any means, electronic, mechanical, photocopying, recording, scanning or otherwise without the prior written permission of Gorgias Press LLC.

2017

ISBN 978-1-4632-0643-7   **ISSN 1935-6838**

```
Library of Congress Cataloging-in-Publication
Data

A Cataloging-in-Publication Record is Available
from the Library of Congress
```

Printed in the United States of America

In memoriam Denis L. T. Bethell (1934–81)

TABLE OF CONTENTS

Abbreviations vii
Preface ix
Manuscripts 1
    Manuscript Transmission 3
    Provenance 6
    Manuscript Description 9
        I. Heading 9
        II. Contents 10
        III. Physical Description 12
        IV. Provenance 17
Textual Criticism 21
    External Criticism 21
        Textual Reconstruction 21
    Emendation 27
    Internal Analysis 32
        I. Authenticity and Forgery 33
        II. Dating a Text 38
        III. Identifying the Author 39
        IV. Sources, Language and Style 42
Editing 45
    Choice of Text 45
    Parts of an Edition 47
        I. Introduction 47
        II. Text 50
        III. Notes 53
        IV. Indices 54
        V. Bibliography 54
        VI. Maps, Charts, and Illustrations 55
Translating 57
    Text 58
    Terminology 58

Personal Names 60
Place Names 61
Bibliography 63

LIST OF ILLUSTRATIONS

Fig. 1. Title page of the Corvina Crysostomos MS OSZK
Budapest, Cod. Lat. 346 viii
Fig. 2. A page from Thietmar's autograph of his *Chronicon* (MS
Dresden R 147)...4
Fig. 3. Colophon of Leiden University MS VLF 5 (s. xiv) 7
Fig. 4. First lines of MS OSZK Budapest Clmae 403 41
Fig. 5. A German Bible translation, Vienna ÖNB Cod.
Vindob. 2760..56

ABBREVIATIONS

CEMT	Central European Medieval Texts (Budapest-New York: Central European University Press, 1998–)
CUP	Cambridge University Press
Ed./eds.	editor/s, edited by
EMC	*The Encyclopedia of the Medieval Chronicle*, Gen. ed. Graeme Dunphy, (Leiden: Brill 2010)
MGH	Monumenta Germaniae Historica
DD	Diplomata
SS	Scriptores rerum Germanicarum
SS rer.Germ.in us. sch.	Scrptiroes rerum Germanicarum in usum scholarum separatim editi
Poet.	Poetae
MPL	Jacques Paul Migne. *Patrologiae Cursus Completus. Series Latina* (Paris 1841–55)
MS/MSS	manuscript/s
trans.	translated by
vol/s.	volume/s

Fig. 1. The Corvina Chrysostomos from Modena (see below, p. 8) fol. 1r, Budapest OSZK MS 346 [with the kind permission of the Országos Széchényi Könyvtár]

Sent as a present of the Duke of Modena to Hungary, it was confiscated in Vienna during the revolution of 1848–9 and reached Budapest only after the end of the Habsburg Empire.

PREFACE

While not all medievalists are faced with the interesting but challenging task of editing a text from one or more manuscripts, it is necessary for those who work with edited texts to know how they came into existence and be able to judge the accuracy of their transmission (or lack thereof). As textual guides are mostly concerned with Classical Latin and Greek (or biblical) manuscripts, a short overview, oriented more towards medieval texts may be useful.[1]

This brief introduction cannot cover the historical, theoretical, and philological work needed for publishing the text of a chronicle or a treatise. However, it outlines the technical steps for preparing a medieval manuscript for print. Its origins lie in a plan to prepare an English-language adaptation of the relevant parts of Heinz Quirin's *Einführung in das Studium der mittelalterlichen Geschichte* (5th ed. Stuttgart: Steiner, 1991)[2] by Professor Denis L.T. Bethell of University College, Dublin and me. Parts of it were ready when Bethell's premature death cancelled this project. The chapter on manuscripts was one such part. It survived and proved to be useful for students of medieval history and culture even in its incomplete form. For a few years, it served as part of a handbook for graduate students at Central European University, Budapest. Then, on the recommendation of Professor Rick Clemens, it was published online in the Digital Commons series of Utah State University,

---

[1] A useful and not overly technical historical background to all of this, is still L.D. Reynolds, G. Wilson, *Scribes and Scholars: A Guide to the Transmission of Greek and Latin Literature*, esp. pp. 186–213 (2d ed., Oxford: Clarendon Press, 1974).

[2] Several passages below, especially on pp. 23–33 are based on that handbook.

whence a number of readers downloaded it, suggesting that it remained of interest. I am grateful to Gorgias Press for having offered to publish a revised and updated version in paperback and to Matthew Steinfeld and his production team for making my sketch into a book. I thankfully acknowledge the aid and counsel of Susan L'Engle (Vatican Film Library, St. Louis), Anna Somfai (CEU, Budapest), and Balázs Nagy (CEU and ELTE, Budapest) in preparing the revised edition.

Budapest, August 31, 2016
J. M. B.

MANUSCRIPTS

The term "manuscript" (MS, pl. MSS) describes a handwritten document from the age preceding the invention of printing. MSS may be in the form of rolls (*rotuli*) but are mostly bound books (*codices*). In what follows we will speak essentially of manuscript books containing the texts of narrative sources,[1] letter collections, saints' lives, legal, scientific, literary, devotional or scholarly texts. Manuscript books are usually kept in libraries. Some are still in the same monastic, ecclesiastical or princely library for which they were copied, but most of them found their way into more or less public collections (see below, pp. 7–8).

Manuscript books are found in a diverse variety of genres and functions from huge tomes of law or science to small devotional Books of Hours.[2] Some general rules apply to all of them, while their specific classes demand special approaches and particular expertise. Due to my experience with chronicle manuscripts, the examples I use are mostly taken from narrative texts from Latin Europe. Manuscripts from other regions and other languages may contain features that require special skills and may have different

---

[1] On these and various issues connected with them (definition, editions, illumination etc.), see *EMC*, passim.

[2] The various genres of medieval Latin and the problems connected to their editing are discussed in the chapters on the varieties of medieval Latin in F.A.C. Mantello and A. G. Rigg, eds. *Medieval Latin: An Introduction and Bibliographical Guide*, pp. 137–183, 241–504 (Washington, D.C.: The Catholic University of America Press, 1996).

conventions, but in general, the procedures described here would apply to those as well.[3]

Medieval codices are also important as physical objects. They offer evidence on the trade and art of the production of books[4] and their writing materials (such as their leaves and inks), as well as on the development of *scriptoria* (copying workshops) and libraries. These aspects are treated by codicologists, and historians of art and of material culture.

Strictly speaking, charters, writs, privileges, administrative and judicial documents are also "manuscripts" (i.e. hand-written). However, deeds and other legal and financial records are a category for themselves. They are as a rule kept in private or public archives. Many of them are still in the keeping of royal, princely, or urban, administrations where they originally served juridical or administrative purposes, often going back to medieval times. These records (even if sometimes in book form) are very different from manuscript books and are treated by the discipline of diplomatics ("the science, which studies the tradition, the form, and the issuing of written documents")[5]—essentially for law, politics, and administration—as well as the form of their sealing (sigillography). I will not discuss them here.

Care should be taken not to confuse similar technical terms in the different disciplines. For example, the provenance of a manuscript refers to the history of its wanderings, and is not to be confused with the *principe de provenance* applied to record sources, which prescribes that archivists should keep records originating from the same administration in their original context.

---

[3] For non-Latin manuscripts there is now a splendid reference work prepared by the research network COMSt: *Comparative Oriental Manuscript Studies: An Introduction*, Gen. ed. Alessandro Bausi (Hamburg: Tredition, 2015), also at: http://www1.uni-hamburg.de/COMST/hand bookonline.html(accessed 10.5.2016).

[4] On these matters, a fine guide is Richard Clement's "Medieval Book Production": http://works.bepress.com/richard_clement/3 (accessed 10.6.2016).

[5] Maria Milagros Cárcel Ortí, ed. *Vocabulaire Internationale de Diplomatique* (ed. 2, Valencia: Collecció Oberta, 1997) p. 21.

Manuscript Transmission

Before a proper judgment can be made about a work and its author, it is first necessary to establish the way in which the text has come down to us, or the *textual transmission*. There are two sides to this issue. One is to find and identify the manuscripts in which the text survived and their history, or the *provenance* (when the text was written, and where, where it was kept, and how it was passed on). The other is to trace the different versions of the text to its earliest ("authentic") form through the various copies extant. The latter will be discussed in detail on pp. 23–33 below.

Very few medieval *autographs* (manuscripts written and corrected by the author himself) are known. We have the autograph of the chronicle of Thietmar of Merseburg with his own corrections, and of William of Malmesbury's *Gesta Pontificum* (with the more scandalous passages struck out with his own pen). Not long ago the autograph of Ranulf Higden's *Polychronicon* was discovered in the Huntington Library in California, and such discoveries are still being made.[6] A noted study was made by Leon M. J. Delaissé of the autograph manuscript of the *Imitation of Christ* by Thomas à Kempis. In what has been described as an "archaeological" examination, he studied it extensively, noting every change to the document.[7] He was able to reconstitute the slow process of its composition, the various changes in the book's plan, and the additions and deletions of text.

---

[6] V. H. Galbraith, "An Autograph MS of Ranulph Hidgen's Polychronicon" *Huntington Library Quarterly* 23 (1959/60) 1–18.

[7] Leon M. J. Delaissé *Le Manuscrit autographe de Thomas Kempis et "L'Imitation de Jésus Christ". Examen archéologique et édition diplomatique du Bruxellensis 5855-61*, (Paris–Brussels: Erasme, 1956).

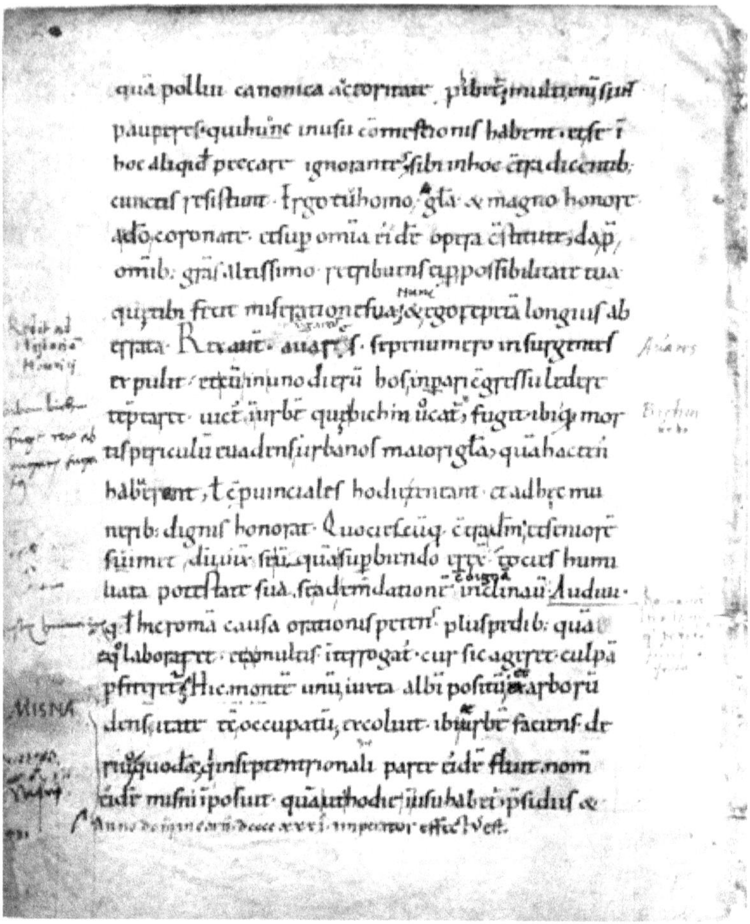

Fig. 2. A page from Thietmar's autograph of his *Chronicon* (MS Dresden R 147)

However, autographs are exceptional. At the other end of the scale are those works which survive solely in fragments or in quotations, or which we know once existed but are now lost. Sometimes reconstruction is possible. One type of evidence is the strips of parchment used to make bindings. A famous case of reconstruction is that of the tenth-century epic *Waltharius*, which began with the recovery of the "Innsbruck fragment," once used by an Ingolstadt binder of the early sixteenth century to reinforce the spine of a book. Other verses were found elsewhere on single leaves, and from these scattered materials, Karl Strecker was able to reconstruct the entire epic.[8]

In between these extremes are the majority of texts that survive in a few manuscripts, usually different from each other at least as regards the copyists' mistakes. Moreover, medieval "editors" frequently added or omitted parts of texts for various reasons: political, aesthetic, technical (space, volume), and so on. Sometimes the authors themselves prepared more than one version in the course of their working life. For example, Cosmas of Prague (d. 1125) wrote separate prefaces or dedications to the first two books of the *Chronica Bohemorum*, which he clearly circulated among friends before putting together the three *libri* of his chronicle.[9]

Then there are authors whose works were immensely popular and of which hundreds of manuscripts survive. It may take years and travel all around Europe—and beyond—to take account of these documents in order to reconstruct the text. Manuscript catalogues help, but they are frequently incomplete.[10] Sometimes medieval texts are found in manuscripts which have been given incorrect or incomplete descriptions or have been given an incorrect title.

Finally, for the sake of completeness, let me add that there are medieval texts that we know only from their printed edition. The manuscript(s) used by the late medieval or early modern editors are lost and, unless they were found, we must rely on the *editio princeps*.[11]

---

[8] *Die lateinischen Dichter des deutschen Mittelalters*, ed. Karl Strecker, MGH Poet. 5.1, pp. 1–79 (Leipzig: Hiersemann, 1937)

[9] See Cosmas of Prague, *Chronica Bohemorum. The Chronicle of the Czechs*, J. M. Bak, P. Rychterová, eds. (Budapest–New York: CEU Press, 2017); see also Lisa Wolverton, *Cosmas of Prague: Narrative, classicism, politics* (Washington D.C.: The Catholic University of America Press, 2015)

[10] There are now a number of manuscript catalogues available on the Internet; for a start, see: http://www.earlymedievalmonasticism.org/Catalogues-of-Latin-Manuscripts.html (accessed 7.5.2016).

[11] For example, the eyewitness account of the Mongol invasion of Hungary in 1241, the "Epistle on the Sorrowful Lament upon the Destruction of Hungary by the Tatars" by Master Roger (ed. & tr. J. M. Bak

PROVENANCE

For a manuscript's provenance, beginning with the *scriptorium* whence it came, we may find evidence in the text itself. To begin with, the handwriting may give a hint to the place and time of its writing. Medieval *scriptoria* (located mainly in monasteries)—where most of our codices were copied—often have characteristic features. With the help of paleography, one may be able to identify the style of the writing that indicates both time and place of writing. However, caution is needed: for example, a scribe using what is called an *insular* script could have been trained in Britain or Ireland, but moved to the Continent retaining the hand he had learned.

For the period before 900 C.E., a census of all known Latin manuscripts appears in E. A. Lowe's *Codices Latini Antiquiores*.[12] It is arranged in volumes by the countries and collections where the manuscripts now reside, gives a plate to show their handwriting; and discusses paleographical questions (for example the abbreviations used) and provenance. For the period after 900 C.E. the number of manuscripts grows increasingly, and studies have become more scattered and regional.

In many cases, there is a colophon at the end of the text or the book, in which a scribe indicates who he is and where he is writing. Frequently such a colophon (especially in earlier manuscripts) consists only of a few words, like *Amen* or *Finis* or *Telos*, perhaps with a short prayer for the soul of the reader or the scribe.[13] However, there are some rather personal ones. At the last leaf (172v) of a Leiden University MS, there are these words: *hoc*

---

and Martyn Rady in *Anonymus and Master Roger*, Budapest: CEU Press 2010 CEMT 5) came down to us only as an appendix to the *Chronica Hungarorum* of Johannes de Thurócz, printed in Brno 1488 (cf. below, n. 2 on p. 50).

[12] CLA=*Codices Latini Antiquiores: A Palaeographical Guide to Latin Manuscripts Prior to the Ninth Century*. Ed. E. A. Lowe. 11 vols. and Supplement (Oxford: Clarendon Press, 1934).

[13] A great collection of colophons was published by the Benedictines of Saint Benoit de Port-Valais, Le Bouveret, *Colophons de manuscrits occidentaux des origins au XVIe siècle*, 6 vols. (Fribourg: Éditions universitaires, 1965–82).

opus est scriptum magister da mihi potum; Dextera scriptoris careat grauitate doloris.[14] Prayer replaced by a drink…

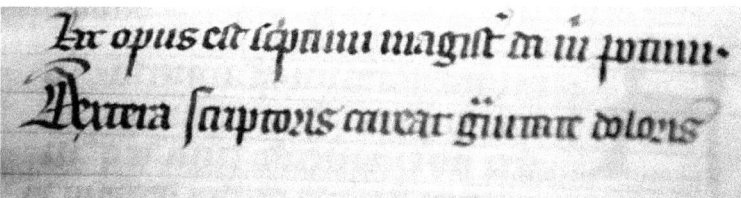

Fig. 3. Colophon of Leiden University MS VLF 5 (s. xiv)

For the further history of a manuscript, there is often an inscription of ownership or shelf mark that indicates that a book belonged to a particular library, in which case the study of medieval and early modern library catalogues is helpful. The Munich scholar Paul Lehmann has done yeoman service in innumerable works on them (notably his editions of the catalogues of Reichenau and St. Gall).[15] In English scholarship, the greatest authority has been Neil Ripley Ker, whose handbook lists all known surviving manuscripts of English monastic libraries, with notes on their printed and unprinted library catalogues.[16] The names of previous owners can also be telling, for they too can act as clues as to where the manuscript originally came from. For example, the name of Dr Thomas Man, who collected many of the surviving manuscripts of the Abbey of Rievaulx, may suggest a Rievaulx provenance. Again, even when we know where and when a manuscript was written, its subsequent history is always important, for it is part of the history of thought

---

[14] See: https://medievalfragments.wordpress.com/2012/09/28/give-me-a-drink-scribal-colophons-in-medieval-manuscripts/ (accessed 13.07.2016).

[15] His works are now collected as Paul Lehmann *Erforschung des Mittelalters* 5 vols., (Stuttgart: Heinemann, 1959–1962). For the later centuries, consult Paul Oskar Kristeller, *Latin Manuscript Books Before 1600: A List of the Printed Catalogues and Unpublished Inventories of Extant Collections*, 4th. Rev. ed. by S. Krämer (Munich: MGH , 1993, MGH Hilfmittel 13).

[16] *Medieval Libraries of Great Britain: A list of surviving books*, ed. 2 (London: Royal Hist. Soc. 1964).

and of collections, and may aid the identification of other manuscripts. Moreover, the fate of a manuscript may shed light on the reception of the given text or texts, their impact on later writings (of those who owned the book or others) and on cultural history in general.

One of the famous libraries of the late Middle Ages was that of King Matthias I (Corvinus) of Hungary (1458–90), the so-called Bibliotheca Corviniana, and its reconstruction has been important for the history of illumination and of Hungarian and Italian Humanism.[17] MS Lansdowne 836 in the British Library has an inscription of ownership, *Ex Bibliotheca Regis Mathiae Dono R'mj Episcopi Quinqueecclesiensis D Antonii Verantij Honor'mi Constantinoplj*. This tells us that Bishop Verancsics/Vrančić of Pécs recovered this copy of Horace, which had belonged to Matthias's library, when he was Hungarian ambassador to the Porte in 1555–7. We can trace it from him through the Dutch collector Gislebertus Cuperus, until it arrived in the library of Lord Lansdowne, who donated it to the British Museum. A Quintilian (now Budapest OSZK Cod. Lat. 414) which was for long time in the Vienna Hofbibliothek has this inscription of ownership: *Liber iste Iohannis Alexandri Brassacani … Bude anno 1525, mensis decembris die 6*. This tells us that it belonged to the Humanist Brassicanus, a Viennese scholar who acquired it in Buda in 1525. He took great care to erase every sign of its previous ownership (only the crown from the coat of arms of Matthias can be seen), but it can still be shown that he had "borrowed" it from the royal library, and that it was made for Matthias in Umbria in 1460–70. A Chrysostom, now also in Budapest (OSZK Cod. Lat. 346) bears the shelf-mark R.4.19. This was its shelf mark in the library of the Dukes of Modena, where it had arrived by 1560. The binding of a Catullus (Vienna, ÖNB Cod. 224) bears the arms of Prince Eugene of Savoy, who received it from the governor of Transylvania. *Habent sua fata libelli.*

---

[17] See Csaba Csapodi, *Bibliotheca Corviniana: The library of King Matthias Corvinus of Hungary*, (Budapest: Corvina, 1981). For an online catalogue, see: http://jekely.blogspot.hu/p/bibliotheca-corviniana.html (accessed 12.1.2016).

In these cases we can follow how manuscripts once made at the orders of a particular patron for his own collection turn up anywhere from Constantinople to St Petersburg, from Budapest to New Jersey. In the case of many less readily-identifiable manuscripts, clues as to its provenance could be any of the indications discussed above: the type of binding, the arms on it, the shelf mark, other manuscripts acquired along with it, and the hands that have scribbled on its flyleaves or margins.

MANUSCRIPT DESCRIPTION

Each manuscript must be properly described before it can be worked upon. Medievalists will most likely be interested in the actual text or texts contained in the manuscript, but a text certainly cannot be edited without a proper description of its manuscripts, and without establishing the text's history of transmission. A good description summarizes a great deal that is important for editors, codicologists, art historians, and others. There is, alas, no generally accepted system for describing manuscripts, but there are good examples of recent scholarly work where authors explain the conventions they have adopted and offer models to follow. Naturally, every group of manuscripts presents its own problems, and may demand special headings to address them. Other manuscripts may simply not supply enough information to permit a full description. The following remarks apply again primarily to the description of Latin manuscripts. Traditional practice in the description of manuscripts in other scripts and languages may vary somewhat, but the basic principles are the same. Essentially, the description of a manuscript must contain four major divisions: (I) heading, (II) contents, (III) physical description, and (IV) provenance.

I. Heading

This identifies the manuscript by its present place of deposit (for example the library or museum), shelf mark, author(s) or title(s), date, language, and a brief note on provenance: e.g. Oxford, Corpus Christi College 209, Augustinus etc., Latin, s. xii/xiii, from Fountains Abbey. The pressmark (also called the shelf mark or call number) usually consists of an internationally accepted abbreviation for the manuscript collection, accompanied by the manuscript's number in that collection. For example:

Clm = Codex latinus monacensis = a manuscript in the Bavarian State Library (Bayerische Staatsbibliothek) at Munich

Cod. Reg. lat. = Codex Vaticanus Reginae Latinus = a manuscript from the library of Queen Christina of Sweden, now in the Vatican Apostolic Library[18]

Guelph. = Guelpherbytanus = a manuscript from the Herzog-August Bibliothek in Wolfenbüttel, the residence of the Guelph (Welf) Dukes of Brunswick, and likely to be one of the manuscripts they obtained with the collection of the bibliophile Illyricus (1520–1575).

An extensive list of MSS of narratives and their abbreviations is found in the EMC 2: 1653–1727, an older guide is F. W. Hall, A *Companion to Classical Texts* (Oxford: The Clarendon Press, 1913.) Such abbreviations should however, be used with caution, and only when they can be presumed to be familiar to likely readers; even then it is essential to include somewhere in the publication a table of abbreviations indicating in full the collections to which they refer.

The date (year or century, the latter usually in Roman numerals with s. for *saeculum*, to which, if appropriate, the specification "early" [in for *ineunte*] or "late" [ex for *exeunte*] may be added) and place of origin should be given briefly even if controversies regarding either or both are later discussed in detail. The language (or languages) are to be noted before or after the summary description of the contents.

II. Contents

Medieval manuscripts are frequently composite (*colligata*) and can contain dozens of unrelated texts. It is only the occasional manuscript that contains one text alone, e.g. Isidore's *Etymologiae* or Augustine's *Confessions* or the Bible. Unlike modern books, manuscripts rarely have a title page, giving the author and the title, and even if they do, this page often refers only to the first work in the

---

[18] The approved abbreviations for Vatican manuscripts can be found on pages vii–x of *Studi i testi* 318.

collection. Since many medieval texts are anonymous, it is of great importance to describe and (as far as possible) identify every single text contained in a codex. It is usual and useful to note the beginnings and ends of texts (Incipit and Explicit) to assist the identification of the text and avoid faulty ascription. Each item of a manuscript should be lettered or numbered. The following information is needed for each, as completely as possible:

1 *Rubrics* (so called because they were written mostly but not always in red, *ruber*) or titles (subtitles) and the beginning and end: Incipit and Explicit. If there is no title given (which is frequent) the three or four opening words are to be given as Incipit, and if these are taken from a classical or biblical text (e.g., in a sermon) the opening words which follow should be added as well.[19]

2 The usual *title* of the work if it does not appear in the rubric, or appears in an incorrect or unusual form in the text. In the rare case, that one encounters a text that has not yet received a traditional title; one should give it a suitable one. Some well-known titles of chronicles and other texts were given them by their first editors—and they stuck.

3 Full cataloguing should include a reference to the *best printed edition* of the text, and note on any major difference from it: gaps, additions, variations in arrangement, or textual variants. This applies only to major differences, whereas detailed differences are to be treated in the course of editing the text. If no printed edition is available, a comparison with other manuscripts is useful, but if this would involve detailed textual analysis, the description is best limited to a summary.

4 An account of any corrections or marginalia, whether early or late, which are of importance for the character and the history of the text. Notes on minor later annotations or corrections which have no textual importance but which may be important for establishing previous ownership belong to IV (Provenance), below.

---

[19] A useful collection of incipits can be found on the site *In principio*: http://www.brepolis.net/pdf/Brepolis_INPR_EN.pdf (accessed 8.23.2016).

The texts in the original nucleus of a manuscript are to be described first. Later additions in margins, on leaves originally left blank, or on added leaves should follow, numbered in the same way as the "original" contents. Their arrangement should reveal—as clearly as possible—the successive stages of the growth of a manuscript as a collection of texts or the uses to which it has been put.

III. Physical Description

The external characteristics of a manuscript are of great importance in establishing its origin and subsequent uses and ownership, and very often serve therefore as the basis for work on texts. It is useful to begin with the actual physical appearance and makeup of a manuscript, i.e., its basic material and number of pages, proceeding on to writing, decoration, and binding, for this reflects the actual making of the book. One needs to consider the process of medieval book production. Medieval codices were not made of sheets of paper folded one or more times, but of pieces of parchment cut more or less to the same size, and folded in half to give pairs of leaves (*bifolia*). These were inserted into each other to form gatherings or quires of four, six or more leaves, and then sewn along the center and bound. In early manuscripts the pages tend to be of unequal sizes, later they were cut after sewing (like modern books), especially when the edges were subsequently gilt. In paper manuscripts the number of leaves in a gathering depends on the number of folds in the original sheet: one fold gives two leaves (folio, abbreviated to 2° or occasionally F°), two folds gives four leaves (quarto, 4°), four gives eight leaves (8°), and so on.[20]

---

[20] On all the technical matters of codicology there is now an excellent (and expensive) handbook by Maria Luisa Agati, *The Manuscript. From East to West: For a Comparative Codicology* (Rome: "L'Erma" di Bretschneider, 2016) including chapters on non-Latin manuscripts. See also: Raymond Clemens and Timothy Graham, *Introduction to Manuscript Studies* (Ithaca, N.Y.: Cornell UP, 2007) or the richly illustrated *Handschriften des Mittelalters. Grundwissen Kodikologie und Paläographie*, Mathias Kluge, ed. (Ostfilden: Thorbecke, 2015).

1   Composition

(a) Number of leaves, including all endpapers or added leaves.

(b) Foliation. Modern books are paginated: i.e., a number is given to each side of every leaf. Manuscript books are normally foliated: i.e., a number is given to the two-sided leaf. The usual reference is to the front of the leaf as *recto* (r) and to the back as the *verso* (v): for example, fol.18v would be p. 38 in a modern book. Some authors use an apostrophe for verso: e.g. fol. 18'. Others use *a* for recto and *b* for verso, but this is not recommended, since the letters *a* and *b* should be reserved for the columns of a page (if there is more than one): e.g., fol. 18vb means "on the second column on the back of folio 18." The form of the Roman or (more usually) Arabic numbers—in a contemporary foliation—may be helpful in dating a codex. (If there is no foliation at all, the cataloguer of the codex should add one.) Previous and mistaken foliation is to be noted. These can be clues to provenance, and to sections now missing or misplaced.

(c) Material on which the manuscript is written i.e., papyrus, parchment (usually membrane or the more refined and expensive vellum), or paper. With paper, one should try to identify the watermarks, as these may assist in dating and identifying the manuscript. A whole literature exists on the subject of watermarks, and there are extensive repertories of them. The classic work by Charles Briquet is still essential, but there are more recent repertoires as well. Some are devoted to a particular type of mark; others are useful for manuscripts from a particular place or period.[21] Even so, it will by no means always be possible to identify a given watermark. Moreover, unless you are fortunate enough to find an exact corre-

---

[21] C. M. Briquet, *Les filigranes*, (Paris: Picard, 1907; repr. 1968, ed. by A. Stevenson); N. P. Likhachev, *Paleograficheskoe znachanie bumazhnykh znakon*, (St. Petersburg, 1899), reissued as *Likhachev's watermarks: An English language version*, eds. J. S. G. Simmons and Bé van Ginneken-van de Kasteele, (Amsterdam: Paper Publication Society, 1994), 2 vols. The Austrian Academy of Sciences has now a program collecting medieval watermarks; see: www.wzma.at.

spondence—and there is a world of difference between identical and similar marks, a fact which Briquet himself did not always appreciate—the most that you will be able to say is that the manuscript was probably written during the (sometimes quite extensive) period during which paper with marks of the type in question is known to have been used.

(d) Materials of the writing. Inks and colors.

(e) Overall measurements of the leaves and the written space usually as height by width, in metric measurements. The format (folio, quarto, etc.) is relevant for books made of paper. (Parchment manuscripts are all technically folios, so in fact no format should be given for them. Nevertheless, for simplicity sake, codicologists often use 4º or 8º for parchment codices as well.) Since the size of papers varied considerably in the medieval period, there is only a tenuous relationship between format and final size; the modern "formats," which really refer to dimensions rather than composition, are to be used only for printed books.

(f) Number of columns and lines. They may be the same on all pages, but not necessarily so. In that case, note the differences.

(g) Collation (or quiring). A parchment manuscript is made of quires. As explained above, a quire is an assembly of pieces of membrane each folded in two and inserted into each other, then sewn together. Two pieces of parchment sewn into each other are a *binio*, three a *ternio*, four a *quaternio*, and so on. Larger quires than *sexterniones* are unusual. Unless there are quire marks (see below, under j), it is not easy to establish the quiring, especially when the manuscript is tightly bound (or rebound). Sometimes the size of the leaves helps, when the margins of the codex have not been cut (that, alas, has happened all too often). A careful look at the codex "from above" can be misleading; finding the threads that hold the quires together is the best method. It may be possible to distinguish bifolia by identifying the inner and outer sides of the parchment; in paper manuscripts, the watermarks, where visible, can be very helpful.

There are different systems of abbreviation for the *collatio* or quiring: e.g. 3 III + VI + 6 IV + 2 III + (IV - 1) describes a manuscript made up of three ternios, one sexternio, six quaternios, two ternios and one quaternio which has a leaf missing. Another, better, system is given below in our example from Neil Ripley Ker, *Medieval Manuscripts in British Libraries*.[22] This, it will be seen, reads "1 10," i.e. the first quire is made of five sheets folded in half, so that f.1 and f.10 are part of the same sheet, as are f.2 and f.9. "6 12 wants 12," means that the twelfth half sheet is missing. "12 two" the quire only has two leaves, and its construction is doubtful.

(h) Arrangement of sheets (i.e., of the hair and flesh sides of the parchment) is not always easy to establish and is frequently omitted even though it may be helpful (for example in establishing origins). It was typical for older insular (Irish, British) manuscripts to have first the hair side of all sheets (abbreviated as HF'HF) and for continental ones—that became general later—like surfaces facing hair outside the first sheet (HF'FH).[23]

(i) Pricking: Small holes made with a needle or a sharp metal tool to guide the scribe who made the ruling. The ruling was made in order to assure parallel lines and (vertically) justified margins. It is rare in early codices, tends to be made by scoring with a metal tool (blind ruling) in the eleventh through the twelfth centuries, and with lead (the precursor of the pencil) from the late twelfth century onwards. Paper manuscripts—and later parchment ones as well—were lined with fine ink-lines, as the sharp tools would have torn the leaves.

(j) Quire signatures and leaf signatures, or *custodes*. These are letters or numbers, usually at the bottom of the verso of the quire's last leaf, or, less frequently, of every leaf, to guide the binder. In the case of leaves, they may be in a sequence such as ai, aii, aiii—but only in the first half of the quire, for the rest follows automatically. Manuscripts were often bound incorrectly, or rebound with quires or leaves missing: the signatures help to show if something like this has happened.

(k) Catchwords. It was often customary to place the first word of the next quire at the bottom of the page preceding it, called *reclamans*. This practice is often to be seen in eighteenth century

---

[22] Neil Ripley Ker, *Medieval Manuscripts in British Libraries*, vol. 1 (Oxford: The Clarendon Press, 1969).

[23] For details, see Clemens-Graham, *Introduction* 131.

books where the catchword (also called *custos*, though inconsistently) come at the end of every page—to help those reading aloud, by saving them from losing the thread as they turned the page. It is usual to note the presence of catchwords in early medieval manuscripts, while in later ones their use can be taken for granted.

2   Handwriting

The description of scripts used for texts, including notes on scribal characteristics, such as letter forms, abbreviations, punctuation and so forth. This is to be solved by a paleographer—a skill of its own.[24] There is often disagreement about the nomenclature of certain kinds of scripts (mainly later medieval ones), and it is wise to cite the authority for one's classification. Note also:

- Guide letters for initials, scribal notes for the rubricator or illuminator.
- Changes of scribe or rubricator in relation to contents or quiring.
- Texts of scribal signatures, mottoes, monograms, etc.
- Notes on the hands of those making corrections and on marginal or interlinear notes made at or near the time or writing.

3   Decoration

Initials, line fillers, border decorations, miniatures. We are nowadays sensitive to the connections between "text and image," the symbolic meaning of colors used, and many other details, therefore, the illuminations and decoration may be of importance for more than just dating and locating the manuscript.

Fully illuminated manuscripts—such as the *Grandes Chroniques de France*—are a class in themselves; their detailed analysis is the

---

[24] For handbooks, etc., on paleography, consult Leonard E. Boyle, *Medieval Latin Paleography: A Bibliographical Orientation* (Toronto: Toronto Medieval Bibliographies, 1984). A more recent summary is by Bernhard Bischoff, *Latin Palaeography: Antiquity and the Middle Ages* (Cambridge: CUP, 1999). A useful bibliography on the subject is found on the site http://medievalwriting.50megs.com/whatis.htm (accessed 5.10.2016).

task of art historians.[25] In the description, a short summary of miniatures, historiated or inhabited initials, and border decorations is sufficient. (See the second example, below.)

4   Binding

Date and origin, technique and decoration. It is especially important, if possible, to date the binding. Later collectors frequently made up composite manuscripts, detached quires and cut margins. Bindings often show evidence of ownership—e.g. coats of arms—that are useful in discussing provenance and may contain hints at textual transmission as well.

5   Opening words of the second leaf

It is unusual to find exactly the same words of the text opening the second recto of a second folio. For this reason, manuscripts were often identified by them in medieval library catalogues (as 2º fol. 4r or similar), and they may serve to distinguish otherwise very similar manuscripts.

IV. Provenance

The brief information given in the heading should be expanded by establishing:

- The original owner or recipient.
- Subsequent owners down to the present.

As mentioned above, evidence is supplied e.g., by type of script, dedications, heraldic devices, inscriptions and marks of ownership, "ex libris," marginalia, liturgical evidence (of use in a certain church or diocese), entries in library or booksellers' catalogues, and references to the manuscript in correspondence. Dictionaries of biography and histories of book collection will help with the identification of owners. References to the handbooks used should be given in footnotes or in a bibliography.

An example may be useful. This is the entry for St. Paul's Cathedral London Ms.3 from Ker, *Medieval Manuscripts*, 242–3. Ker

---

[25] See, e.g., the articles on illumination in EMC 1: 843–71.

explains his conventions in his preface, and it is useful to consult them.

3. Avicenna   s. xiv in. 1. ff.
1 - 502 v Incipit liber canonis primus. quem princeps abohali abuisceni de medicina edidit. verba abohali abuiscenni. In primis deo gracias agemus . . . (f.2^v) Dico quod medicina est sciencia . . . kerates xxviiii.

Avicenna, Canon medicinae, in five books in the translation of Gerard of Cremona. Often printed : GKW 3114-24. A few leaves are missing and the leaves of quire 27 are out of order : see below. Tables of contents in front of bks. 1 and 4, which like bks. 2 and 3, but not 5, begin on new quires : part of the table of bk. 4 has been copied twice. The colophon of bk. 5 is in a current hand in the margin of f.502^v as a guide to the rubrics or, who did not copy it, however, in the space left for it after 'kerates xxviiii' : so far as it can be read it agrees nearly with B.M., MS Royal 12 G. vi. Contemporary notes refer to another copy, e.g. (f.77^v) In al' nones'. Annotations of s. xiv, xv in English hands include seven lines of verse on f. 389 : [F] leubotomus, uentus, scarpellus, caute, sacellus . . .

2. ff. 502^v--3 Qui abscidunt sanguinem menstruorum . . . ad tinnitum aurium. Explicit liber Quintus Deo Gracias. A collection of recipes which commonly follows the Canon and is here treated as part of it. A reference to it follows the colophon of art. 1 in the margin of f. 502^v : Liber hauch (?) filli hysaac sic completus est liber.

3. ff. 503--7^v Alfachimid est medicus . . . Zegi id est atramentum. Expliciunt sinonima auicenni.

4. ff.507^v--8 Aced genus absinthii subalbidi . . . Nelem id est meituritilis (*read* mercurialis). Expliciunt exposiciones secundum arabicos et secundum almasorem.

An alphabetical table of materia medica ending at N. It follows art.8 in Merton College, MS 224 - where it ends at L - and in Erfurt MS F. 247. ff.v+420+iv, foliated (i-v), 1-209, 300-402, 402*, 403-43, 443*, 444-508 (509-12). 360 x 260 mm.

Written space 250 x 168 mm. 2 cols. 57-64 lines.

Collocation 1^{10} 2^8 $3-5^{12}$ 6^{12} wants 12, blank, after f.65 $7-11^{12}$ 12 two (ff.126-7) $13-14^{12}$ 15^{10} 16 nine (ff.162-70) $17-22^{12}$ 23^{12} wants 6 after f.340 (ff.336-40, 335, 341-5) 24^{12} 25^{12} wants 6, 7 after f.362 26^{10} 27^{12} (ff.379, 378, 380, 321, 381-4, 322, 385, 387, 386) 28^2 (ff.388,389) 29^{12} 30^8 31^{12} 32^{10} $33-34^{12}$ 35 two (ff.454, 455) 36^{12} 37^{10} wants 6, probably blank, after f.472 $38-39^{12}$ 40^{10} wants 9, 10, probably blank.

Signatures I-XXXIX and a medieval foliation ending in bk. 4 date from a time when bk. 2 (ff.66-127) was misbound at the end. Two hands, the second writing bk. 2 and the last quire but one.Initials : (i) of each book (ff.2^v, 66, 128, 394, ink of the text occasionally marked with red. Binding of s.xix. Secundo folio *doctrine principiis pertinet* (f.3).

Written in England. The gift of John Somerset in 1451 : f.65v (cf.f.127), 'Hunc canonum

Magnum Auicenne Philosophi pocius quam medici. ut patet ex principio primi libri ex sui ipsius Relatu et probamine Canonem videlicet speciose consideracionis Et graciose composicionis Emptum per me de *domp*no Iohanne Rectore Ecclesie Sancti Michaelis in Wodestrete London'. (John Smith, rector 1447, d.1473). Ego Magister Iohannes Somerseth Arciumliberalium et artis Salutigeri Doctor. Cancellarius Scaccarii Anglie do concedo et delibero librarie Ecclesie Sancti Pauli London" ibidem munde et secure custodiendum pro perpetuo ad Ecclesie catholice Ihesu cristi commodum et honorem. Hec Cirographice pando nono die maij Anno regni regis Henrici Sexti post conquestum. Vicesimo nono Deo Gracias. Hec Somerseth' (*the last two words in red*). Entered as D(1) in the catalogues of 1458 (ed. Dugdale, *History of St. Paul's Cathedral*, 1658, p. 277): Avicenna in Canone 2^0 folio *Doctrine principiis pertinet*. No. 169 in Young's catalogue, c.1622.

Or here is another one, for general information, from the Cambridge Digital Library, abbreviated from: *Western Illuminated Manuscripts: A Catalogue of the Collection in Cambridge University Library* by Paul Binski and Patrick Zutshi, with the collaboration of Stella Panayotova, Cambridge, 2011 (you will see that the details of quiring are omitted; that can be done)

Cambridge University Library **Classmark:** MS Ee.3.59
[Vita S. Eduardi, regis et confessoris]. La estoire de seint aedward le rei translatee de latin
Author: (Matthew Paris, 1200-1259)
Place, date, language: England, London/Westminster c.1250-1260; Old French
Former Owners: Eleanor, Queen, consort of Edward I, King of England, d. 1290; Nowell, Laurence, 1530-ca. 1570; Lambarde, William, 1536-1601; Cope, Walter; Burghley, William Cecil, Baron, 1520-1598; Moore, John, 1646-1714; George I, King of Great Britain, 1660-1727

Sole extant copy of verse Life of St Edward the Confessor probably by Matthew Paris, composed for Queen Eleanor of Provence, using post-translation vita by Aelred of Rievaulx and Matthew's own historical works. Contrary to CDDMC, no. 24, only date of composition of lost original may be ascertained, 1236-72, probably 1236-45, perhaps 1236-39 (Binski, 'Abbot Berkyng's Tapestries', pp. 89–95). This manuscript is a London-Westminster copy, perhaps made for Queen Eleanor's daughter-in-law Eleanor of Castile on her arrival in England in 1255. Possibly one of the books about Sts Thomas and Edward repaired and rebound for Queen Eleanor of Castile in 1288 (wardrobe account in National Archives E101/352/11 mem. 2, see B.F. and C.R. Byerly, Wardrobe and Household, p. 379, no. 3217). List of liberal arts (19v lower margin). At least three artists. Manuscript may be compared with three related Apocalypse MSS from same workshop, New York, Pierpont Morgan Library MS M.524 (compare 3v-5r), BL Add. MS 35166, Los Angeles, John Paul Getty Museum, Ludwig MS III and Oxford, Bodleian Library MS Tanner 184 (compare 5v-6r) (Morgan, Survey, nos 122,

124–25 and 107), the present manuscript being the latest in style and the most heterogeneous. Related also to wall paintings of c. 1250 in the Dean's Cloister, Windsor Castle.

Editions: Luard, H. R., *Lives of Edward the Confessor*, (London: Longman, Brown, Green, Longmans, and Roberts, 1858).

Wallace, K. Y., *La estoire de seint Aedward le Rei* (London: Anglo-Norman Text Society, 1983).

La Estoire de Seint Aedward le Rei (Oxford: Roxburghe Club, 1920)

Extent: 37 fols (f. 35 missing), Leaf height: 279 mm, width: 193 mm. (102-177-112 x 165 mm)

Material: Parchment

Binding: Full green morrocco (Douglas Cockerell & Son, Grantchester, 1967).

Script: Gothic bookhand (cursive)

Layout: 3 columns (2 on 36), 48 lines to full column (13-26 below miniatures), ruled in plummet, below top line, rubrics, catchwords, 2o fol. *pur purchater* (4r)

Decoration: Forty-two framed drawings over all three text columns and twenty-two over two, some containing more than one scene, tinted in blue, green, red, pink and brown, many with inscriptions, some rubbed, with occasional details in gold (14v, 19v, 20r) and fictitious heraldry in battle scenes (5r, 12r, 12v, 31r, 32v, 34r, 34v).

Ornamental and minor initials: Opening ten-line initial A (should be C) in blue and gold, with red penwork flourishing, added 14th or 15th century C.E. (3r); alternating red and blue penwork flourished initials (2-3 lines).

Border decoration: A few bas-de-page drawings by main artists: heads of man and woman kissing below commentary on theme of chastity, faces rubbed out (3r) with illegible red caption in hand similar to or identical with some captions in pictures (e.g., 30r, 32v); vines and oak leaves tinted in green and brown (13v, 14v, 16v, 20r) or only sketched out (36r); sketch of eagle's head (28r).

Provenance: Perhaps Eleanor of Castile; Laurence Nowell, antiquary, 1563 (3r), perhaps acquired from William Bowyer, Keeper of Records in the Tower, who made numerous manuscripts available to Nowell (Black, 'Laurence Nowell', p. 117 and n. 7); William Lambarde, friend of Nowell (ibid., 116) (3r); 'Mons. Cope' (3r, i.e., Sir Walter Cope, d. 1614; see A.G. Watson, 'Sir Walter Cope' (MS B2)); perhaps William Cecil, Lord Burghley, d. 1598 (apparently sold with other books from his Library (T. Bentley and B. Walford, 21 Nov. 1687)); John Moore (d. 1714); presented to University Library by George I, 1715.

Textual Criticism

Once the manuscripts—in this context usually referred to as "witnesses"—have been assembled, the texts have to be critically sifted and evaluated. There are two major steps in this process that results in establishing the best reading of the text: external criticism and internal criticism. The former is more technical and can be described in relatively general terms. The latter is less suitable for a short summary.

External Criticism

External criticism treats the state of the text from a formal point of view. The questions it asks relate to the various relationships between the different parts and states of the text (e.g., in different manuscripts or redactions), how independent they are from each other, and, if necessary, whether the text is genuine. The main procedure is the comparison of as many versions of the text as possible in the attempt to survey the entire breadth of the textual tradition. It has the two aims of establishing a text which best reflects the intentions of its author, and reconstructing the history of the text's use and transmission. (Here, once more, codicology and textual criticism uses a different term from diplomatic works, where "external criticism" relates merely to the parchment or paper, the writing, and the sealing.)

Textual Reconstruction

As we have already discussed, autographs rarely survive. Quite frequently neither does any manuscript closely related to the autograph.

Essentially, we wish to obtain a text that is as near as possible to the "original," to the author and his/her time. The surviving witnesses must therefore be examined and arranged in order. This is achieved by the comparison of the manuscripts in order to decide which has the best surviving texts. How independent are the witnesses of each other? And, therefore, how genuine are they?

There are two main approaches—one may call them schools—to deciding which text should be the most authentic and thus the basis of an edition. One approach is known as "recensionist," the other as "optimist" (not referring to a positive view of the future, but to the *textus optimus*, as will be discussed below).

Recensio is the procedure of reconstructing the most authentic text (closest to the original), traditionally called the *Archetype*. In this procedure, the relationship is established by a comparison of the different readings and, based on mistakes and other peculiarities, sorting out the less authentic ones. Karl Lachman (1793–1851), the pioneer of critical text editing in nineteenth-century Germany (where he worked on both biblical and Old High German texts) is usually credited with having established this method. In fact, he built upon concepts as old as the Humanists.[1]

The process of comparison begins with collation. The easiest way to do this is to write the text in the different witnesses out in columns, so that differences in readings (or agreements) can be seen. Divergences and differences between different manuscripts may be marked in colors. Thus it can, for example, readily be seen that "red" manuscripts are different from "blue." But red and blue are perhaps more closely related together than a "green" group (which can be recognized by the mistakes which a transcriber made in his exemplar, and which have been carried on downwards in its different copies). Such groups are then ordered by resemblance into *classes* and *families*, derived in different ways from the archetype. This family relationship is called *filiation*. Much of this can now be done electronically on the computer and there are special programs that help doing it.[2] Such a classification enables us to decide on the

---

[1] For a discussion on the origins of the method and a critical survey of it, see Sebastiano Timpanaro, *The Genesis of Lachmann's Method* (Chicago and London: University of Chicago Press, 2005).

[2] An interesting blog on this matter, referring mainly to modern literature is: William Raabe, Collation &c. http://wraabe.wordpress.co/2008/07/26/collation-in-scholarly-editing-an-introduction, listing a

worth of different classes of manuscripts and their probable reliability.

Omissions and interpolations are the best means of determining the relationship between manuscripts. (Other variants may arise independently in different manuscripts!) A manuscript with a given portion of the original text cannot have been copied from one that lacks it. Lost manuscripts will be christened (as in mathematics) with symbols like X, Y, Z, (for the unknown). The result can usually be expressed in what is called a *stemma*. The families can be identified by capital letters: A, B, C, etc.,—and for their members it will be most convenient (and memorable) to use the initial letter of the manuscript's name (from the place where it is kept). For example, I for the Innsbruck fragments, K for the manuscript in the Karlsruhe Landesbibliothek, P1 and P2 for the two manuscripts from Paris.

As an example here is the stemma of *Henrici Chronicon Livoniae*, eds. Leonid Arbusow and Albertus Bauer, MGH SS. rer. Germ. in us. schol. 31, (Hanover: Hahn, 1955)

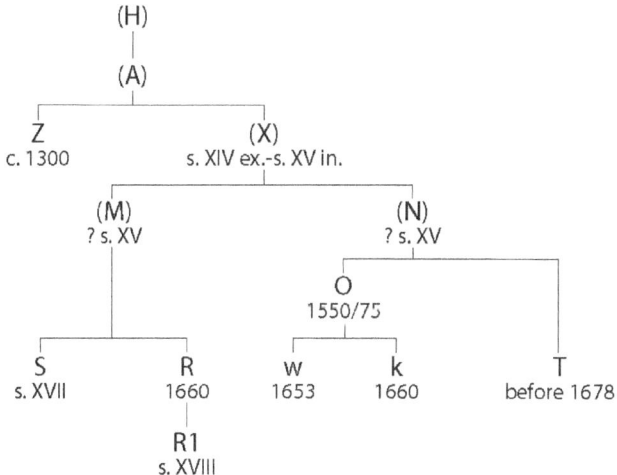

---

number of useful links (accessed 5.7.2016). There are other guides and discussions online.

(H) Lost original of the author (H)enry (ca. 1225–7).
(A) (A)rchetype of the now surviving MSS None of the other MSS derive from Z. But they share readings with Z which cannot be those of the author, because there are nonsensical words or obvious omissions. Therefore Z and all other MSS derive from an unknown intermediary manuscript which was not Henry's own
Z Codex **Z**amoscianus (Zamoyski Library, Warsaw): Cod. membr. c. 1300

Z is a good text, preserving readings lost or corrupted in the other witnesses, but a careless copy, with large gaps which the other MSS do not have. Further mistakes were imported into the texts belonging to the group deriving from (M) and (N), both now lost, but otherwise independent. Their common exemplar must have been another copy of (A), which is therefore called (**X**).

(M) an assumed fifteenth-century transcript that was the model for the three following witnesses sharing common interpolations and omissions:
S From the **S**kodiesky collection in the Riga town library, Stadtbibliothek Riga 2394. Cod.chart. (paper MS). A careful copy of the seventeenth century.
R Library of the Gymnasium in **R**eval (Tallinn) MS III 98 Cod.chart. A poor transcript from c. 1660.
R1 copy of R from the eighteenth century, used by J. G. Arndt, the first translator.
(N) a postulated copy of (X) which was better than (M), and the model for the following two MSS as they share the same readings and interpolations:
T **T**oll collection, Reval (Tallinn), now in the Estonian State Archives. It was commissioned and excerpted by the historian Thomas Hiäarn who died in 1678
O Niedersächsische Landesbibliothek Hanover MS.XXXIII 1746. Cod.chart. from the **O**xenstierna collection initially. Written in Livonia by a sixteenth century Humanist. He made interpolations using books published in 1550 and 1552, and his work was used by an antiquary in 1575.

Two late copies dependent on **O**, of no value for textual reconstruction (hence given lower case sigla):
w Stadtbibliothek Riga 2482. Cod.chart. Written by Johann **W**itte in 1653.

k   Estonian Association of Learned Societies,
Dorpat MS 250. From the **K**nüpfer collection,
written by two scribes in Stockholm in 1660.

Conclusion

Z should be the basis for the edition. When Z fails, S is the next best witness; since O and T have been so much interpolated and revised that they should be considered only when S fails.

Several reservations can be made about constructing stemmata. In many cases, the history of transmission is unclear, and no one missing "X" can be safely postulated as the intermediary between the extant witnesses and the missing archetype.

Maurice Bévenot put his finger on this difficulty when he wrote:

> The construction of such a stemma depends on a certain view of the transmission of MSS: it adopts as basic the obvious fact that a copyist makes mistakes, and that his mistakes will be copied by the next generation or give rise to fresh mistakes. Thus MSS get worse down the centuries, and therefore when we are postulating ancestors, we must suppose them to have been better and better up the centuries as we get nearer and nearer to the author himself.[3]

Bévenot was dealing with the writings of Cyprian, a patristic author, whose works were widely spread, and who received a great deal of early medieval edition, including a great deal of emendation and contamination. While in the case of some groups of manuscripts stemmata can be constructed and manuscripts eliminated, a whole group of manuscripts will be left whose readings are equally strong; and while on the basis of them a text can be established it would be too much to say that an archetype ever can be. Indeed, in the case of Cyprian's *De Unitate*, the variants are so strong that it is not too much to suppose (though we cannot prove) that Cyprian himself issued a revised version, and for certain passages the texts

---

[3] M. Bévenot, *The tradition of manuscripts: a study in the transmission of St. Cyprian's treatises* (Oxford: The Clarendon Press, 1961).

can only be printed parallel as alternatives. In others the manuscript tradition will certainly not allow us to rule out a reading, and if it is to be discarded it cannot be on grounds of philology or manuscript tradition, but only on the basis of what we know of Cyprian's own way of thinking—a judgment which is bound to have an element of the subjective.

Then, the history of a given text can cause other problems in constructing an archetype. Medieval books were "published" in the sense that authors could and did circulate them—sometimes in portions as the Prague canon did.[4] Authors worked over their texts, altering them and adding to them even after the first transcriptions had been made. Controversial texts in particular were likely to be copied *in statu nascendi*. Who can today possibly decide between the variants of such texts?

As mentioned before, the alternative to the *receptionist* or Lachmann-tradition is the Bédier or *optimist* method.[5] It is based on the principle that we wish to have a text of a medieval work that was in fact read (listened to), learned, quoted—in a word, used—by a medieval (and early modern) public. Let us remember that the rigorously (re)constructed archetype in the best MGH tradition is a text which we do not know whether it was ever read by anyone. (A text polemically referred to by some as a "test-tube text".) In contrast, we may decide to search for a version of the text that can be proven to have been in circulation in several copies, and ultimately we may choose the one of which most copies survived (or are

---

[4] See above, n. 10.

[5] Joseph Bédier (1864–1938) worked mainly on French vernacular texts, above all on *chansons de geste*. He "defended" his method in "La tradition manuscritrite du *Lais del'ombre*. Reflexions sur l'art d'éditer les anciens textes" *Romania* 54 (1928) 161–96, 321–56—note that he called his work an art! On the two traditions, see A. Castellani, *Bédier avait-il raison? Le methode de Lachmann dans les éditions des textes du moyen âge,* (Fribourg: Presses Univ., 1957) and Leonard E. Boyle, "Optimist and Recensionist: 'Common Errors' and 'Common Variants'?" in: *Latin Script and Letters A.D. 400—900. Feschschrift Presented to Ludwig Bieler on the Occasion of His 70th Birthday,* John O'Meara and Berndt Neumann, eds. (Leiden: Brill, 1976) 264–74.

known to have existed, for example from medieval library catalogues or from frequent quotations in other works or other references). Then we would edit that text, verbatim (in what is known as a "diplomatic edition"). It may be still useful to note the variants in other manuscripts (or groups of manuscripts) if we want to present a truly critical edition, but the main body of the text will be taken from one manuscript (or group of manuscripts) which we have reason to believe were widely received by medieval audiences and readers. This procedure seems to have gained ground in recent decades, not unconnected with the growing interest in the reception of texts and in their impact on the public for which they were written. One, therefore, might call this approach a "functionalist" one. As far as I can see, it is applied most frequently to literary texts, poetry, romances and related genres.

EMENDATION

Once the text has been established, it may require emendation in places where a scribe or series of scribes have made a mistake. Manuscripts were either copied from other manuscripts or, frequently, written down from dictation. For original works, an author often wrote his draft on wax tablets, which he might either copy out himself or give to a scribe. In all these processes mistakes can readily occur. As anyone will understand who has tried to copy a text himself, texts are easily miscopied. They were even more easily misheard, and a dictator was likely to introduce glosses into the text. In such cases, emendation becomes necessary, the grounds for it are those of grammar and sense, and their justifications are paleographical, grammatical, and literary. A helpful, but not unproblematic principle is that of the *lectio difficilior lectio potior*. This rule was pronounced as early as by Erasmus of Rotterdam in editing biblical texts and has been applied mostly to biblical and classical works. It is relevant when there are (two or more) different sets of readings of which one is more "difficult," or less usual than the other. This principle presumes that scribes tended to simplify the text, replacing less well-known or "complicated" words by simpler ones. Therefore, the more difficult one may be the original. For instance, for the Life of St. Wulfric of Haselbury there are four manuscripts: F and H have *macerabat*, E and C read *mactabat*.[6] Both words have—among other things—more or less the same meaning: to slaughter, to kill. However, the former is used in this meaning rather rarely, thus, considering the elegant style of the author; we may suspect that the less educated scribe chose a more common version. The former may thus have been the original.

It is, however, important not to impose our own cultural presuppositions in the application of the principle of *lectio difficilior*: what is *difficilior* for us may have been the more familiar possibility for the scribe. Nowadays the principle is debated; above all by those who prefer actually read (*optimum*) texts to (Lachmannian) reconstructed ones. Among them, Martin L. West wrote:

> When we choose the 'more difficult reading' ... we must be sure that it is in itself a plausible reading. The principle should not be used in support of dubious syntax, or phrasing that it would not have been natural for the author to use. There is an important difference between a more difficult reading and a more unlikely reading.[7]

Moreover, one should not try to correct the author under the guise of amending a faulty copy.

Emendation is based on a presumption that some form of corruption crept into the text, as a result of bad transcription, laziness or ignorance. It should never introduced tacitly: all editorial interventions must always be signaled, lest the reader be left with the impression that the emendation is the actual text of the manuscript. This can be done essentially in two ways. The amended form can be printed in the body of the text and the original—faulty, incomplete, different—text added in a note, with reference to one or more witnesses containing it/them. This is the traditional "MGH-style" procedure and is appropriate when a composite text (based on the stemma) is being presented. Alternatively, the

---

[6] Life of St. Wulfric of Haselbury, ed. M. Bell, *Sommerset Record Society* 47 (1933) 67.

[7] Martin L. West, *Textual Criticism and Editorial Technique applicable to Greek and Latin texts*, p.51 (Stuttgart: Teubner, 1973).

"faulty" text can be printed, especially when the edition follows the "Bédier method" and presents one "best" manuscript, and the annotation will contain a reference to the "correct" form: *recte*: &c. However, every editorial project has its own particular style and that has to be applied consistently.

Traditional emendation results mainly in the removal of expansions, interpolations, and corruptions.

1   Expansion

It is very common for explanatory or additional remarks of one kind or another to come into texts, not necessarily for any reason of bias. e.g. *Tertia via ad idem (in qua deducitur Virginem peccatum originale non contraxisse) sumitur ex peccati originalis indecenti macula*, in Hermanni de Scildis, "Tractus de conceptione gloriosae virginis Mariae". The scribe of Ms. K added the words in parentheses to explain what the author was doing.

2   Interpolation

Interpolation means deliberate alteration by expansion (or deliberate omission). For instance, there are two versions of the basic constitution of the Cistercian Order, now known as the *Carta Caritatis Prior* and the *Carta Caritatis Posterior*. When the two are compared, there is a clear case of interpolation in the clause on visitations carried out by the Abbot of Cîteaux: *Semel per annum visitet abbas maioris ecclesiae (per se vel per aliquem de coabbatibus suis) omnia coenobia quae ipse fundaverat, et si fratres amplius visitaverit, inde magis gaudeant.*

The words in parentheses come from the Posterior. They were plainly interpolated at a date when the number of houses founded by Cîteaux had become large and the abbot had to delegate his duties to fellow abbots.[8]

---

[8] See: *Les Plus Anciens Textes de Cîteaux*, ed. J.de la Croix Bouton (Achel: Abbaye cistercinne, 1974) [Commentarii Cistercienses Studia et Documenta 2].

3   Corruptions

The following (with examples taken mostly from Burchard of Ursberg's *Chronicle*),[9] are the common kinds of corruption:

(a) Omission

Dropping either a word or a line (particularly common in poetry and extremely helpful in establishing stemmata). For example, there are three manuscripts, A, B, P of Otto of Freising's *Gesta*: the passage in parentheses has been omitted by A:

> *Libra (casei octo denariis emebatur; caro carissima erat. Nam in) quarta parte bovis mortui dedi XX soldos et unum.*[10]

(b) Homoioteleuton.

This means jumping from one similar sounding letter, syllable, or word to the next. For example:

> *Lotarius quoque imperator eo modo confortatus est in imperio (nam et supra dictus Cuonradus, qui ei adversabatur in imperio) a facie eius ierat in Italiam.*

In Ms. A of Burchard the passage in parentheses is missing. (p.14). Plainly, the scribe's eye jumped from one *imperio* to the next.

(c) Dittography

The repetition of a letter or a syllable: e.g. *lattere* for *latere* (Burchard, p.2).

Care should be taken here, for medieval spelling was not classical spelling. Certain duplications found their way from the vernacular pronunciation into the texts or, in turn, double consonants were dropped, because the vernacular speaker did not "feel" the difference. Both can be valuable clues to the author's (or scribe's) background.

---

[9] Burchard of Ursberg, *Chronicon*, MGH SS rer. Germ. in us. schol. 16.

[10] Otto of Freising, *Gesta Frederici imperatoris*, MGH SS rer. Germ. in us. schol. 46, 50.

(d) Transposition
Transposition of letters, words, and phrases is common, and in poetry whole verses are frequently copied in the wrong order:

> ... *filii Eginonis comitis de Urach quorum Curradus postmodum conferesse ad ordinem Cisterciensem (fuit abbas Cisterciensis) indeque per sedem apostolicam translatus fuit Romae episcopus cardinalis Portuensis videlicet et Sanctae Rufinae* (Burchard, p.81).

The scribe of MS.A omitted the phrase in parentheses. Having done so, he tacked the words on to the end of the sentence.

(e) Mistakes in reading and word division
The scribe of MS.A wrote *olim ad vie* instead of the correct *olim a dive* (p.15), *vel in more* instead of *vel minorem* (did he mishear what was being dictated to him?) (Burchard, p.32).

The scribe of MS.P has the nonsense *sal in me bibi* (in an inserted letter of Innocent III). He overlooked the abbreviation marks in his original: the correct reading is *salutem in medio terre*.

Abbreviations are a common cause of trouble: e.g. those for per, pro, and prae. So are minims, as in *minimum*. These mistakes will vary with the type of script being copied: e.g.: if a scribe confuses pr, rn, ns, if he writes *hoc* for *autem*, the odds are high that he is copying from an "insular" manuscript.

(f) Such mistakes give rise to "bungling improvement"
For example, the marginal glossator of MS.P above realised that *sal in me bibi* is nonsense, and corrected to *salvator in medio terre*. (Burchard, p. 100).

The scribe of MS.A has *inierunt* for *iverunt*. The manuscript he had before him probably had *iuerunt*. What must have happened was that the scribe read the word as *inerunt*, found it ungrammatical, and corrected to *inierunt*. (Burchard, p. 222).

(g) Contamination
This does not mean full-fledged interpolation or insertion. It applies to a case where a scribe has two or more manuscripts of the same text in front of him, which contain variant readings that he

then includes indiscriminately. For example, Adam of Bremen's history of the Hamburg bishops has:[11]

filia regis Danorum apud Michilenburg, civitatem Obotritorium, inventa cum mulieribus, nuda dimissa est.

The scribes of manuscripts B and C have instead of *nuda dimissa* an alternative: *diu caesa*. Albert of Stade (author of *Annales Stadenses*, MGH SS 16) obviously had two manuscripts in front of him and wrote *diu caesa nuda dimissa est*.

If a passage is hopelessly corrupt an editor must use an *obelus* (†) to indicate that she/he thinks so. Or write (*sic*) to indicate that the text is incomprehensible and no easy emendation can be offered.

INTERNAL ANALYSIS

Internal criticism deals with a text's contents and studies the text's special characteristics and the author's methods and motives. At this stage, it concentrates on the particular nature of the one source under review. Concerning historical or scholarly texts the major aim used to be to decide what worth the source had as evidence for events or theoretical positions, but now questions that are more sophisticated are also asked. Scholars scrutinize texts for the author's educational background, political loyalty, his (or her) handling of the traditions (*memoria*), the purpose of writing (*causa scribendi*) and many others.[12] Most of that belongs to the field of literary, historical, theological or scientific analysis of the text and cannot be easily summarized. A few questions—more or less "technical"—can still be discussed.

---

[11] Magistri Adam Bremensis, *Gesta Hammaburgensis ecclesiae pontificorum*, 194, entry for 1066 (ed. 3, Hanover: Hahn 1917, MGH SS rer. Germ. in us. sch. 2).

[12] See, for instance, Gabrielle M. Spiegel, *The past as text: Theory and practice of medieval historiography* (Baltimore: Johns Hopkins UP, 1997) and several articles of hers.

I. Authenticity and Forgery[13]

Is the text what it says it is? The problem is of course a central one regarding charters but can and should be asked of other texts as well: whether our source is what it appears (or is presented) to be on grounds of form and content. Forgery of manuscripts—especially of narrative or literary texts—is quite rare, except, for example, in so-called cartulary chronicles that are prone to contain forged or interpolated deeds. Decisive arguments will emerge from an analysis of the contents, but some formal criteria (not unlike those used in a diplomatic text) may prove useful.[14]

To begin with, one should not confuse issues of "veracity" with forgery. Chronicles, for example, may contain false dates, consciously (e.g., to prove an early date for the foundation of a town or a monastery) or because of insufficient information.

Confabulations, be they mythical or otherwise invented, serving the interest of a certain person or group, do not constitute forgery. For example, soon after the publication of the anonymous *Gesta Hungarorum*, the learned Paul Schlözer denounced it as a "fable" because the data on the early medieval Rus' principalities were wrongly given. He regarded it as a forgery, although there is no doubt that it was written in the Middle Ages, most likely in the early thirteenth century (see n. 29 on p. 44). The critique of such matters belongs to the literary analysis of the source but not to the *distincio veri ac falsi*.[15]

It is important to distinguish between forgery by a contemporary and forgery or alteration by a later hand. A later forgery can be detected by comparison with undoubtedly genuine texts. Writing materials, ink, script, and language should be compared. Style analysis can be used, but cautiously, for it is by no means infallible. Anachronism may be telling. The text must be examined for lacunae, and whether these are deliberate, or the mere oversight of a

---

[13] On the general issue of medieval forgeries, see now the six-volume collection of articles: *Fälschungen im Mittelalter* (Hanover: Hahn, 1988, MGH Schriften 33: 1–6) esp. vol.1.

[14] On these, see EMC 1: 256–9.

[15] On this matter, see e.g. Franz-Josef Schmale, "Fälschungen in der Geschichtsschreibung," in: *Fälschungen* as above, 1: 121–32.

scribe. The question of motive must be gone into, for it will often lead to insights well beyond the mere detection of forgery.

A star case of a literary forgery and the unmasking of a forger is the *Vita* of Bishop Benno II of Osnabrück, (1068–1088). The text was edited by Rogerus Wilmans in MGH SS 12, and rests on witnesses none of which are older than 1666. (That is not necessarily a bad thing. The age of a manuscript is no guide as to whether its text is good or not. It depends on the scribe and on what he was copying.) Friedrich Philippi soon attacked its genuineness.[16] Paul Scheffer-Boichorst (1843–1902), one of the most learned scholars of his time, replied with arguments on grounds of medieval philology that, while admitting some tampering with the text, vindicated the *Vita* as such.[17] He held that the core of it was genuine, but not five chapters contained in it, which had visibly been composed on the basis of the foundation charters of Iburg. Shortly after Scheffer-Boichorst's death, Harry Bresslau found a collection of manuscripts on Osnabrück history dating from the mid-seventeenth century in the city archives of Cologne, one of which contained a text of the *Vita*. It differed from that printed in the *Monumenta* in a number of places—most notably, in omitting the five chapters whose authenticity had been doubted by Sheffer-Boichorst. Bresslau edited it in the *Monumenta*,[18] and demonstrated (among other things) that the genuine text still existed at Iburg in 1652, and a newer one was prepared a little later. It was plainly related to a quarrel between the then reigning abbot, Maurus Rost, and the bishop of Osnabrück in 1666 about the bishop's rights over Iburg. Verbal resemblances could be found between the five chapters and some annals written by Abbot Rost, and this makes it

---

[16] Friedrich Philippi, "Norberts Vita Bennonis eine Fälschung?" *Neues Archiv*, 25, 1900, 767–96.

[17] Paul Scheffer-Boichorst, "Norbert's Vita Bennonis Osnabrugensis episcopi eine Fälschung?" *Sitzungberichte der kgl. Preussisches Akademie der Wissenschaften in Berlin*, 1901, 132.

[18] *Vita Bennonis episcopi Osnabrugiensis auctore Norberto abbate Iburgensi*, ed. Harry Bresslau. MGH SS rer. Germ in us. school. 56 (Hanover: Hahn, 1902)

certain that he was the forger whose work was transcribed in the manuscripts used by Wilmans, which certainly existed by 1683.

Another celebrated case of interpolation is in the text of Asser's *Life of King Alfred*, which received attention from a number of forgers, but nowhere more obviously than where the historian and herold William Camden (1551–1623) who inserted a passage to vindicate the antiquity of the University of Oxford. The learned Archbishop James Ussher (1581–1656), pronounced against it immediately, but it was over a century before the forgery was admitted by the University.[19]

It will be noticed that both these examples are from the seventeenth century and that in the first, we are dealing in effect with an elaborate charter forgery. When charters occur in literary texts, there is room for suspicion: mentions of legal privileges may be interpolations. Saints' lives were occasionally written—or rewritten—in this spirit. Deliberate interpolation can often be spotted in an original text by the fact that it is written over an erasure. Often an erasure does not leave sufficient room, and the writing is cramped. Sometimes the interpolator tries to imitate an older hand, and he naturally does not have the ductus of the genuine hand.

However, outright medieval forgery of literary texts or chronicles is decidedly uncommon. Less devious interventions are more usual. The process of copying or dictation, the inclusion of a gloss into the main body of a text may enlarge or change it; texts could be barbarously edited (just as today); authors revised their own work or collaborators did so; and polemical treatises were changed to fit new cases. But direct literary forgery is rare. To be sure, elaborate fictions were dreamt up, sometimes deliberately concocted. Geoffrey of Monmouth cannot be called a "forger," although he foisted a mythical history on Britain which is not dead yet. So, more solemnly, did the monks of Glastonbury, whose unceasing attempts to provide their ancient church with a good set of relics

---

[19] In his 1603 edition of the *Life*, he has this sentence: "In the year of our Lord 886, the second year of the arrival of St Grimbald in England, the University of Oxford was begun ...". Camden may have "inherited" this forged passage from a certain Henry Savile, known as Long Harry (1570–1617).

eventually led to the preposterous tales of Joseph of Arimathea and Arthur, with a full scale interpolation in William of Malmesbury's *De Antiquitate Glastoniensis Ecclesiae*.[20] But, again, we are in the world of claims to privileges.

Claims that a historical text is forged should be advanced with the greatest care and the strongest presentation of motive and justification. In 1870, Paul Scheffer-Boichorst published a fundamental essay attacking the genuineness of the earliest Florentine vernacular chronicle, the *Istoria Fiorentina*, which purported to be written by Ricordano Malispini and continued by his nephew or grandson Giacotto.[21] He compared its text with that of Giovanni Villani's famous *Nuova Cronica XII libri* (written about 1345) and concluded that the *Istoria* was a late fourteenth century forgery, based on plagiarism from Villani. In sum, the events in the *Istoria* which are not in Villani are designed to enhance the reputation of the Bonaguisi family, to whom the Malispini were related. It credits them with an ancient history (a Bonaguisa was the first to scale the walls of Damietta, and so on) and stresses their connection with more ancient houses. Scheffer-Boichorst began a scholarly controversy that lasted for a century. In 1969 the question seemed to be settled by Charles T. Davis.[22] Scheffer-Boichorst was correct in suspecting the *Istoria*: none of the alleged authors can be unequivocally identified but seem to have lived in the thirteenth century (where the story ends, in 1286) and much of the text depends on Villani. The final judgment is that it "has to be re-dated to the second half of the fourteenth century" (V. de Aprovitola in: EMC 2: 1062) and thus the claim of its being the oldest vernacular chronicle is untenable. Why then did it take a century before his conclusions were accepted? First, in the last century, no manuscripts of the *Istoria* were known, and while Scheffer-Boichorst's textual analysis was exact and careful, he did not in fact search for the witnesses that were to be decisive. Secondly, his study would have required a

---

[20] Now best in J. Scott, ed. and trans., (Woodbridge: Boydell, 1991).

[21] Paul Scheffer-Boichorst, "Die florentinische Geschichte der Malaspini eine Fälschung," *Historische Zeitschrift* 24 (1870) 274–313.

[22] "The Malispini Question," *Studi Medievali* ser. 3, 10 (1969) 215–54.

closer analysis of Florentine family history. Thirdly, while great respect is due to so great and perceptive a scholar, Scheffer-Boishorst had two weaknesses. He presented his conclusions in a tone of triumph of German scholarship over Italian nationalism and emotionalism, and he was too eager to believe that men liked to forge and to plagiarize. This prejudice led him on to question the *Cronica delle cose correnti ne' tempi suoi* of Dino Compagni (c. 1246–1324).[23] If the *Istoria* was indeed forged, then Compagni had the next claim to be the earliest Florentine historian writing in Italian. Scheffer-Boichrost noted that Compagni got many of his details wrong, and suspected another case of over-credulous Italian patriotism, and of later forgery. However, he himself discovered a commentary on Dante written in 1343, which had extensive passages taken from Compagni. After an extensive controversy with Isidoro del Lungo,[24] he had to admit that Compagni was genuine, and that it was rash to try to date Italian vernacular texts without the assistance of scholars of early Italian.

Yet if here he was mistaken, and not least in the tone of his writing, Scheffer-Boichorst was right in pointing to the fact that national pride and prejudice have been in modern times an important motive for both forgery and the acceptance of fakes. A good example is the group of poems from early medieval Bohemia "discovered" by the Czech Slavist Václav Hanka in 1817 in the famous Königinhof Manuscripts (*Rukopisy královédvorské*). These forgeries played an important role in the "Czech national awakening." The learned František Palacký remained to the end of his life unwilling to admit that this "evidence" of a glamorous and free Slav

---

[23] Ed. Ludovico Antonio Muratori, *Rerum Italicarum scriptores* 9 (Milan, 1726) 467–536; online: https://it.wikisource.org/wiki/Cronica_delle_cose_occorrenti_ne'_tempi_suoi (accessed 11.07.2016); English transl. D. E Bronstein, (Philadelphia: Penn. U. Press, 1986) An older transl. by E.C. M. Benecke and E. G. Ferrers (London: Dent, 1906) is online as: https://archive.org/stream/chronicleofdinoc00comp#page/10/mode/2up (accessed 11.07.2016).

[24] Isidoro del Lungo, *Dino Compagni e sua cronica*, 4 vols. (Florence: Le Monnier 1879–87; e-book ed. 2015).

past and a better poetry of the Czechs than the Germans was nothing but a figment of Hanka's imagination.[25]

II. Dating a Text

Most of medieval texts do not state when they were written. The criteria for dating them are then internal and external. Internal criteria come from the contents: e.g. if the author narrates a personal experience, or if he/she gives details that make it plain that she/he was an eyewitness. That can give a *terminus post quem* for the author must have been writing after that date. It is most helpful when we can date events mentioned in the text from other—preferably record—sources.

Astronomical dating can be useful as it is most reliable; for example, if the author mentions a solar or a lunar eclipse that can be checked in the *Five millennium catalog of solar eclipses*.[26] But we must remember that what we have is again a date *post quem*.

The *terminus ante quem*, the date before which he must have been writing, is a good deal more difficult to determine. For example, suppose the text has "the present king Alfonso." That places the passage after Alfonso's accession: but Alfonso may have died before the author wrote down the final version of his draft; or he may be copying a previous author. Very often, the best one can arrive at is to place a source merely in a certain range of dates.

For example, the biographer, Walter Daniel, tells us that St. Aelred of Rievaulx wrote his treatise entitled "When Jesus was twelve years old" before sickness compelled him to retire to a special cell. We know that that happened in 1157. There is nothing else in the treatise to date it by. Aelred certainly wrote it as a Cistercian (and therefore after 1134). His language suggests that he was an abbot at the time he wrote (therefore after 1143). Walter implies

---

[25] From the extensive literature (mostly in Czech and German) on these forgeries, see Pavlina Rychterová "The Manuscripts of Grünberg and Königinhof: Romantic Lies about the Glorious Past of the Czech Nation" in: *Manufacturing a Past for the Present: Authenticity and Forgery in Nineteenth Century Texts and Objects*, J. M. Bak, G. Klaniczay, P. Geary, eds. 1–30 (Leiden: Brill, 2015).

[26] http://eclipse.gsfc.nasa.gov/SEcat5/SEcatalog.html

that he wrote it at Rievaulx (therefore after 1147). He mentions the treatise after he mentions Aelred's *Genealogia Regum Anglorum* which has the incipit *Ante tamen hoc tempus* and then the one beginning with *Eciam ante illud tempus* ("When Jesus was Twelve"). Now, however, we can date the finishing of the *Genealogia* to between 24 May 1153 and 25 October 1154. It seems reasonable then to date "When Jesus was Twelve" to between 1153 and 1157.[27] In other words, we have a definite *terminus ante quem*, but not certain, though a reasonably plausible *terminus post quem*.

III. Identifying the Author

There are many texts for which we do not know who the author was, or even in what century it was written or where. Lacking the author's name may be partly due to the Christian command of humility, partly to the often-complicated textual transmission.

Linguistic evidence can be helpful, though it can be dangerous and linguistic experts can change their minds (e.g. the shift of a number of undated Middle Irish texts back from the twelfth century to the tenth!). It is especially important for vernacular texts where traces of pronunciation can be detected: e.g., a Middle High German scribe who wrote *chaiser* for *kaiser*, *Lotag* for *Dienstag*, and repeatedly replaces b with p, is undoubtedly a Bavarian. If he writes *brengin* for *brengen* and *abir* for *aber*, he is rather more likely from central Germany.

Script may betray an author's nationality (e.g., Anglo-Saxon script is unlike anything written on the contemporary continent, but Anglo-Saxon scribes can be found working, inter alia at St. Gall as well). Expert knowledge of scripts and scriptoria is needed to determine this correctly. A tenth-century leaf of parchment survives of Widukind of Corvey's *History of the Saxons*. Its script is minuscule, and it is folded as a contemporary of Widukind's would have folded it. Still it cannot be the autograph. The monastery

---

[27] *The Life of Ailred of Rievaulx by Walter Daniel* ed. F.M. Powicke, (London: Nelson, 1950), xci, xcvii, 39, 41; *Quand Jesus eut Douze Ans*, 13 (Paris: Cerf, 1987) [Sources Chrétiennes 60].

school of Corvey did not teach its students to use the script in which it is written.

In a wider sense, the text may point to a certain intellectual surrounding. For example, one may be able to compare the literary quotations in a text with the (often known) holdings of a certain monastery or cathedral (or even university) that may suggest the author's readings and thus his or her place of writing—or at least study. But this kind of inquiry leads us already to more complex aspects of internal criticism.

Much scholarship was applied to remove the "anonymous" adjective from the title of medieval writings. Especially in the eighteenth-nineteenth century scholars insisted on identifying an author for major works that may very well have been written by several authors (such as monastic annals). Discussing these efforts concerning the oldest narrative of Rus' history, that was finally—without good reason—ascribed to a known monastic author from the Kiev Cave Monastery, Oleksiy Tolochko asked ironically when did "Nestor" write the chronicle? He found that it was in the mid-eighteenth century that the statesman and historian Vasilii Tatishchev decided upon Nestor's authorship to get way from the anonymous adjective. It stuck.[28] The aforementioned *Gesta Hungarorum* faired better (or worse?): after 200 years of attempts at identifying its author, "he" is now simply called the Anonymous, and has a statue in the City Park of Budapest, with the face hidden. The author identifies himself in the first words of the text merely as: *Pdictus magister ac quondam bone memorie gloriosissimi bele regis Hungarie notarius…*

---

[28] Oleksiy Tolochko, "On 'Nestor the Chronicler,'" *Harvard Ukrainian Studies* 29 (2007) 1–31.

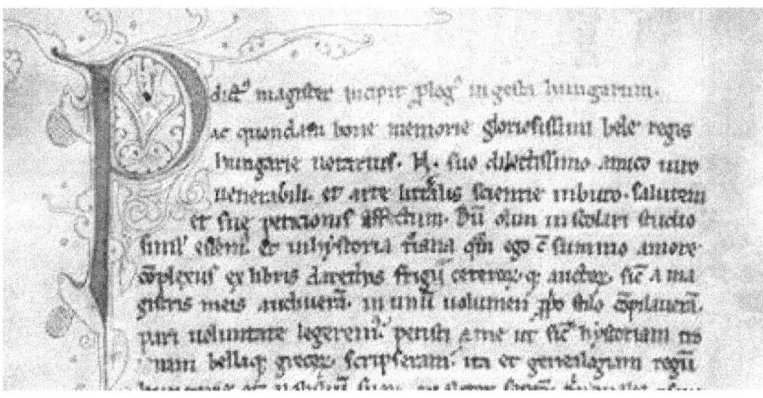

Fig. 4. First lines of MS OSZK Budapest Climae 403

Now, there is no full stop after the P, thus it was suggested that it is an abbreviation for Prae/Predictus, implying that there was some kind of title page, where he was named. The surviving *manuscriptum unicum* (OSZK Budapest Clmae 403; late thirteenth century, not autograph) has no title page—and that would be in any case a rarity for the earlier Middle Ages. Thus, the author could not have been "aforesaid." Then, all efforts were made to find a person with a name beginning with P in the probable time of writing, assuming that it is an abbreviation for Peter or Paul or some similar name. This was unsuccessful. But there is more to it. If not *predictus* than the author calls himself *dictus magister*, "master by name"? Meaning what? Mere humility *topos*? Then, he was the former (retired?) notary of King Béla. Very well, but there were four Hungarian kings by that name: one in the eleventh, two in the twelfth and one in the thirteenth century. Who was the former master of the writer? After a library full of controversy, the present consensus is that he was in the court of King Béla III (1173–96), and wrote his *Gesta* around 1210. For this, innumerable bits and pieces of the text were consulted, the attitudes of the author to certain events, his topographical knowledge, his mentions of certain persons, and other indicators of time and space scrutinized.[29]

Sometimes one may try to identify the author on a statistical analysis of his/her style and use of language. This is promising, when there is some hypothesis about an author whose other works are known. The procedure is an exacting task, though in the age of computers less difficult than it was previously.[30] One starts out by making statistics of the frequency of certain words used in the anonymous text and compares it with the statistics of other texts. This is called a *stylometric* analysis.[31] For example, a Polish scholar recently did such a study on the chronicle of the so-called Gallus Anonymous, ca. 1118. ("Gallus" because the first editor suspected a French monk was the author.) With quite complicated network analysis, he established it was likely that the author was a certain Venetian, Monachus Littorensis, whose authorship had been suggested by earlier scholars. The results are open to debate.[32]

IV. Sources, Language and Style

This part of editorial work is least suitable for a short summary as it is less a technical matter than one of literary, historical and theoretical considerations. The procedure will very much depend on the character (genre) of the text and the concerns of the editor.

It is commonplace that medieval authors were not concerned with being original, rather, the use of highly regarded old texts—

---

[29] Anonymi Bele regis notarii Gesta Hungarorum/Anonymus, notary of King Béla, The Deeds of the Hungarians, ed. and trans. Marty Rady and László Veszprémy, in: *Anonymus and Master Roger* xix–xxiv (Budapest-New York: Central European University Press, 2010 [CEMT 5].

[30] For the history of the method, see Harold Love, *Attributing Authorship: An Introduction* pp. 14–31 (Cambridge: CUP, 2002).

[31] A good introduction is Efstathios Stamatatos, "A Survey of Modern Authorship Attribution Methods", *Journal of the American Society for Information Science and Technology*, 60 (2009), 538–56.

[32] See Maciej Eder "In search of the author of Chronica Polonorum ascribed to Gallus Anonymus: A stylometric reconnaissance", *Acta Poloniae Historica* 112 (2015) 5–23. Available online: http://www.aph-ihpan.edu.pl/images/112_01_Eder.pdf (accessed 09.07.2016).

from the Bible through the Classics and Church Fathers—was considered a virtue. The notion of plagiarism is a modern one. Establishing the verbatim or edited quotations from previous texts is important not only to show the learning (and intellectual surroundings) of the author, but may contribute to decisions about authorship, date and location. With the internet, resources for finding the origin of a clause or set of words is now much easier than before. There are a number of online concordances to the Bible and other texts.[33] Nevertheless, an editor has to be well versed in the Bible and the Classics so as to be able to recognize implicit quotations. Familiarity with Christian liturgy, which most of our (clerical) authors knew by heart is a forte.

For historical texts, the sources may be several. Chroniclers borrowed freely from earlier narratives or from classical authors. In theological or legal treatises, famous authors as "authorities" are quoted with or without credit to their origin. That should not impeach their authenticity. It is common view that Einhard, characterizing Charlemagne with words borrowed from Suetonius, selected such clauses that fitted his subject, so that he may very well have presented the person of the emperor truthfully. It was somewhat less convincing when Cosmas of Prague copied almost verbatim the eulogy of Regino of Prüm on Louis the German (died 876) and his queen Hemma for Prince Boleslaw II (d. 999) and his wife with the same name as Louis'. Maybe this parallel moved him to do so.

Chroniclers often based their more extensive coverage on terse annals or reflected oral traditions. This is a subject for itself. Moreover, so is the selection and presentation of past events, depending on both the concerns (or biases) of the authors and the

---

[33] For example: the Clementíne Vulgate Project (http://vulsearch.sourceforge.net/cgi-bin/vulsearch); or the ARTFL Project (https://www.lib.uchicago.edu/efts/ARTFL/public/bibles/vulgate.search.html) for the Latin Bible. For both Classical and Medieval Latin, the best is Brepols's Library of Latin Texts A and B (http://www.brepolis.net/pdf/Brepolis_LLT_EN.pdf [by subscription]). For the Douay-Rheims translation across from the Latin Vulgate, see http://www.latinvulgate.com/ (all accessed 20.7.2016).

gaps of memory. Nowadays *memoria* is a central issue of scholarship.[34]

In mentioning the language of the text, we mean the type of Latin (or otherwise) the author uses. The grammar and style will likely add to the dating and localization of the text as well as to the literacy and education of the author. Not only do scripts point to a particular "school," but also matters such as certain forms of declension and similar features. (On stylometry, see above.)

Textual analysis should also include matters that belong to medieval rhetoric and style, for example, the presence of fictive speeches (*sermonisatio*), rhymed prose, poetic inserts (*prosimetrum*), and many more. These aspects go beyond this introduction.[35]

---

[34] See, for example, Mary Carruthers, *The Book of Memory. A Study of Memory in Medieval Culture* (Cambridge: CUP, 1990).

[35] For issues of style and rhetoric, see, among many others, the online English translation by R. H. Johnson of Dag Norbert's *Manuel pratique de latin médiéval* (Paris, 1980): http://www.orbilat.com/Languages/Latin_Medieval/Dag_Norberg/index.html (accessed 09.07.2016) and Mantello-Rigg, *Medieval Latin* as above, n. 2. on p. 1.

Editing

The problems and necessary decisions in editing[1] a text are considerable and I have mentioned them in several contexts above. What follows are a few aspects which are relevant to the study of the editions we already have, and to the initial steps in preparing a new one.

Choice of Text

First, one has to decide what kind of edition is appropriate to the text at hand. If there is only one known manuscript (MS *unicum*), the decision is easy: it has to be transcribed, freed from any obvious scribal errors, and edited with an appropriate introduction (on which below). In the rare case of an autograph manuscript, there are certain specific problems. In transcription and edition, one must follow the original with particular care. The author's own special characteristics of spelling should be noted, e.g. whether he uses the *e caudata* for *ae*, and for which words. For example, Eadmer, who did use it but not for *saeculum*, *aemulus*, and *aestimo*.; and he regularly spelt *cumque* and *namque* with an n. Such things are important for establishing his linguistic and educational background. It does not follow that his usages need to be reproduced in

---

[1] Anyone planning an edition, should read the booklet of the well-known Latinist-editor (of William of Tyre and many others), R. B. C. Huygens, *Ars edendi* (Turholt: Brepols, 2000). Subtitled "A practical guide to editing medieval Latin texts," it is in fact a charmingly subjective admonition of master to pupil, with many a practical hint at avoiding pitfalls while editing. See also Idem, "Looking for Manuscripts ... and Then?" at http://www.illinoismedieval.org/ems/VOL4/huygens.html (accessed 14.07.2016).

the final text, but they must be noted and briefly discussed in the introduction. A few "modernizations" are nowadays tacitly accepted, so, for example, to change the u to v in such cases as *auus* to. *avus*, but not every edition does this. (It should be noted in the Introduction, whether one does it or not.) It is also extremely important to note, but not necessarily follow, the author's punctuation (see below).

When an original autograph does not exist, and there are several manuscripts available, the first decision is whether one opts for the traditional method of establishing a text that is assumed to be as close as possible to what the author wrote, in classic phraseology, to "restore the Archetype." The methods for doing so have been described above. The Lachmannian tradition is derived from the practice of editing classical literary texts. No originals exist for them; the texts nearest the originals are very rare, and confined to late and frequently unreliable witnesses. The learned editor of such texts could normally be fully confident that he knew more of the language and methods of their authors than did the scribe of the late manuscripts. Even so, the process of textual criticism of classical texts is far from being reducible to a series of purely mechanical processes, and no one would assert that the editing of them is finished and that there is nothing more left to be done; or that the solutions to the "best" reading of what was originally written are purely philological. To correct the work of a poet requires a poet's sensitivity to language, and some alternatives are bound to be chosen by subjective instinct.

We have already discussed the difficulties of constructing a stemma in the situation where a very large number of variants exist, or when a work has been copied at different stages in its writing. A less difficult form of the problem is very common, where we have two-three variations. The one solution is a variorum edition in which the major versions are printed in parallel columns or some similar arrangement and it is left to the reader to decide which reading is preferable. Another option (the Bédier principle) is to print the text as it stands in one particular manuscript. If we have any indication that that manuscript (and/or its close "relatives") was the most widely used version, i.e., the text that may be taken to have had the greatest impact on contemporaries and later readers, it may make good sense to print that one, regardless of its corruptions vis-à-vis the assumed but unknown "uncorrupted" original.

On the other hand, we may have witnesses all of which are late and of approximately equal value. Here an "eclectic" text can be established. The "best reading" must be chosen in the sense that the language of the author, the literary practice of the time of writing (as far as they can be conjectured) should be represented correctly. Such a process puts less emphasis on the "grammatical norm" and the "philologically correct" than on what is "individual" and "unusual" in the author's own use of speech and genre. Editors of medieval documents are not only grammarians or literary critics: their task is to approach the text historically and produce an edition that is as true to the author's writing as possible. That does not of course mean supplying archaic spellings that none of the manuscripts contain!

PARTS OF AN EDITION

The parts of a good edition and the conventions for the presentation of the text are in all cases quite similar: it has to have a good introduction, a clearly printed, easily readable text, critical annotations and other aids to the user, including as many indices as possible and appropriate.

I. Introduction

The Introduction has two main functions: first, to summarize for the reader all that is known about the text (its author, its transmission, its contemporary use and survival) and second, to clarify the procedure by which the editor arrived at the format presented in print. In some series editors have opted for introductions in Latin, thus making the prefatory remarks accessible to all those who would be able to handle the text. Unfortunately, this has gone out of fashion and by now it is a rarity to find a Latin preface (and Latin commentaries). Even the MGH SS abandoned this practice, and print now the corollary matter in German. Most recently, however, the new critical edition of Johannes Thuróczi's *Chronica Hungarorum*

(1488) has a Latin preface and an entire separate volume of critical comments in Latin.[2]

I believe that the MGH editions may still count as the standard for the structure of the Preface (at any rate for historical works), consisting usually of four major parts:

1   The author

The character, length, and critical detail in this first chapter will depend even more than the rest on the given text. If the author is well known and his/her work extensively discussed in the scholarly literature, the presentation of the author will not have to be long when supplemented by the relevant bibliography in the notes. However, if there are new insights, gained, for example, from the newly edited text or other sources, or if the author and the work are less well known, a detailed biography with special reference to the edited text will be appropriate. It should also discuss the writing's place in the author's life, the author's social or political position while writing, his or her attitude to the events, and so on. Naturally, if an anonymous text is in the edition ascribed to a person, the reasoning for having done so has to be presented in detail.

2   The work(s)

Whether the edition contains more than one work of the author or not, it is useful to place the edited text in the context of his/her entire literary activity, including the relationship of the works to each other. If several works are edited, all of them have to be discussed in the sequence as they are printed. The discussions of dating (under circumstances with reference to the author's biography), the character of the work, its value as a source (authenticity, point of view, originality, etc.) and its contemporary or later medieval (and modern) reception belong here. The use of the text by later writers may receive a special chapter if the work was especially

---

[2] Johannes de Thurocz, *Chronica Hungarorum*, I. *Textus*, eds. Elisabeth Galántai, Julius Kristó (Budapest: Akadémiai Kiadó, 1985); II. *Commentarii* 2 vols. eds. Elemér Mályusz, Julius Kristó, (ibid. 1988) [Bibliotheca Scriptorum Medii Recentisque Aevorum, S.N. 7–9].

influential and had many followers. Similarly, the sources of the author, the authorities used; the relationship to classical or earlier medieval authors should be noted. The analysis of language and style also belongs here. Some editors include an itemized list of the quotations from the main sources, the Bible, and classical literature; the grammatical peculiarities; cases of rhymed or rhythmical prose (such as the so-called *cursus*),[3] and poetic inserts. That may be sometimes unnecessarily extensive.

3   Manuscripts and editions (translations)

This is the place to survey all the known manuscripts of the work, both those witnesses that were used for the edition and those not accessible to the editor (or lost and known only from references). The manuscripts have to be described according to the scheme outlined above (or at least in an abbreviated form of manuscript description if they are otherwise known from good descriptions in modern catalogues). The witnesses and their use for the edition are to be discussed and the decisions of the editor as to the priority of texts explained (either by reference to a reconstructed stemma or by arguing for some other procedure). If there are earlier drafts, a discussion of the different versions (by the author him/herself) and their relationship to each other belong here. It may be important to evaluate critically early printed and other previous editions; for they may contain information on manuscripts now lost or editorial decisions, which the present editor approves of or wishes to revise. If there were medieval vernacular (or other language) versions or early modern translations, they should certainly be listed, for these, too, may contain hints to the history and influence of the text. Further, it is useful to list (and consult) recent modern translations, for those may also contain additional critical notes, interpretations (every translation is an interpretation!) and scholarly comments. It may make sense, depending on the textual history, to discuss the later use of the text here, and to follow its "afterlife" in other au-

---

[3] For a quite technical discussion, see Sven Eklund, "The use and abuse of cursus in textual criticism," at: documents.irevues.inist.fr/bitstream/handle/2042/3361/02%20TEXTE.pdf (accessed 05.05.2016).

thors and/or in historiography or scholarship, Humanist and modern.

4 Arrangement of the present edition

Having presented the arguments for the selection and structure of the edited text, in this last chapter the editor should explain the technical details of the procedure followed, the conventions used, the system of the critical apparatus, and all editorial decisions. For example, in the recent edition of the letters of Hildegard of Bingen the editor decided to add two kinds of textual notes: an *apparatus comparatiuus* and an *apparatus criticus*.[4] Since there are variants of the letters in collections overseen by Hildegard or corrected by her, the variants in these collections are listed in the first set of notes, while the second group contains the usual textual comments based on *emendatio* etc. It never goes amiss, either, to explain one's procedure as to the marking of dates (on the margin) or the page/folio numbers of earlier editions or of the major manuscript, even if these follow received practice.

II. Text

The text should be printed in standard letters (usually 12 pt) with wide margins. Some early editorial projects printed ancient texts in a specially designed archaic character set (e.g. the English Record Commission series). Such a practice, of course, is mistaken, as the purpose of the edition is precisely to make the text, written in a hand not easily read by everyone, accessible to the modern, paleographically untrained user. Passages that are verbatim taken over from another text—including the Bible and the Classics—are usually set into italics or petit (10 pt), or if there are different major blocks of borrowing, one of them can be set s p a c e d. In such a case, the origin can be marked on the margin or in a footnote. The margin can be used also for marking the actual date to which the passage or entry refers (especially in chronicles or histories), regardless of the source's dating it, or dating it wrongly. If it appears nec-

---

[4] *Hildegardis Bingensis Epistolarium*, Pars I, ed. L. Van Acker, (Turnholt: Brepols, 1991, Corpus Christianorum Continuatio Mediaevalis 91).

essary, the folio of the original manuscript (esp. in the case of editing from an autograph or a specially important manuscript) can be marked either within the text, usually [in brackets], or on the margin of the printed text, with a line signifying the exact point of page break.

Punctuation is a difficult part of any edition.[5] The intention of Latin's classical punctuation (as described by Donatus) was to give direction to the reader, who was expected to be reading aloud. Three punctuation marks were recommended, the *distinctio*, *media distinctio*, and *subdistinctio*. All these had the form of a modern full stop/period, and were distinguished by their height above or below the line. The *distinctio* marked the end of the sentence and was written above the line. The *media distinctio* marked a point about midway in a sentence where breath could be taken, and it was written on the line. The *subdistinctio* was below the line, as its name implies, and indicated a breathing point where little of the sentence remained. The disadvantage of this system was that it required considerable delicacy in placing, gave considerable difficulty to transcribers, and did not indicate rise and fall in emphasis. The results were first, the collapse of all stops into the *media distinctio*, and second, the elaboration in the Carolingian period of two stops. The first was a point for pause and breath in a sentence where pitch was sustained, thus : (like the modern colon) and second to show where at the end of a sentence the voice was lowered, thus ; (like the modern semicolon). In the thirteenth century, Thomas of Capua called these signs the *comma* and *periodos*.

The indiscriminate use of the *media distinctio* or medial stop is likely to give rise to the mistakes of the transcriber/editor. A famous example is in the text of Bede in his description of the death of King Penda at the battle of the Winwaed: *Inito ergo certamine fugati caesi pagani, duces regii XXX, qui ad auxilium venerant, pene omnes interfecti; in quibus Aedilheri, frater Anna regis Orientalium Anglorum, qui post*

---

[5] An excellent treatment of this matter is available in M. B. Parkes, *Pause and Effect: An Introduction to the History of Punctuation in the West* (Farnham: Ashgate 1992). A brief overview by Diana Tillotson is online as http://medievalwriting.50megs.com/scripts/punctuation/punctuation1.htm (accessed 25.04.2016).

eum regnavit, auctor ipsi belli, perditis militibus siue auxiliis interemtus est.[6] There has been a great deal of scholarly speculation as to why King Aethelhere of East Anglia should have caused the war. But, in fact, Plummer's comma is a mistake. J. O. Prestwich demonstrated that the text should read: "... *qui post eum regnavit. Auctor ipse belli* ..." Penda started the war.[7]

This example may be enough to show that considerable care has to be given to an author's or a manuscript's system of punctuation. It was considered part of the teaching of style in the Middle Ages and *Artes punctuandi* were attached to the *Artes dictandi*. When an autograph manuscript exists, there may be good reason to reprint an author's punctuation (as has been done in the Oxford Medieval Texts by Richard W. Southern for Eadmer and Marjorie Chibnall for Orderic Vitalis).[8] Nonetheless, the basic rule remains that punctuation should serve a modern understanding of the text as established by an editor who has considered its meaning and style. Generally, the earlier a manuscript the more care its punctuation requires, for in monastic manuscripts it is more likely to reflect the author's. Systems of punctuation underwent considerable changes in the Middle Ages: our own system derives from the Italian Humanists of the fifteenth century.

It is widespread usage to number the lines on each page for easier reference (and sometimes used for the critical apparatus as well), usually on the inner margin. In poetry the line numbers often go through an entire section (part, canto, etc.), in prose they start anew on every page. Sometimes the line numbers include the notes as well, sometimes only the text. The inner margin can be used, for example, to indicate the folios of the witness or the page number in

---

[6] *Bedae Venerabilis Historia ecclesiastica gentis Anglorum*, III, 24, Carolus Plummer, ed. 2 vols., 1, 178 (Oxford: Clarendon Press 1896; repr. several times).

[7] John O. Prestwich, "King Aethelhere and the Battle of the Winwaed" *English Historical Review*, 83 (1968), 89–95, here. 92–3.

[8] R.W. Southern, ed. and tr. *The life of St Anselm, archbishop of Canterbury*. (2nd ed., Oxford: Oxford University Press, 1972); Marjory Chibnall, tr., *The Ecclesiastical History of Orderic Vitalis*, 6 volumes (Oxford: Oxford University Press, 1968–1980).

an earlier, widely used edition, in order to facilitate reference to, for example, the MPL or the MGH.

III. Notes

The *apparatus criticus* (usually in the form of footnotes, i.e., notes on the bottom of the page) consists of three kinds of commentaries: variant readings (if there is more than one manuscript), references to allusions and borrowings, and explanatory remarks on the contents. It is MGH convention to use lower case characters (a, b, c,) for the variant readings and numbers (1, 2, 3) for explanatory or critical notes. The textual notes refer to the manuscripts used by capital letters (cf.the abbreviations for a stemma, as above). A frequent abbreviation is *om.* for "omitted in" which may refer to several words missing in a certain manuscript (or group of manuscripts), in which case a–a, b–b is the best way to mark the passage. *Add.* stands for "added in" when a word or passage in a manuscript (or manuscripts) was not included in the edited text.[9] *Lacunae* (empty spaces) or truncations in the texts (caused, for instance, by a tear in the parchment, burns, missing leaves) should also be marked in these notes. Explanatory notes may cover various things. They may refer to authorities used verbatim or in paraphrase by the author; in the latter case cf. (confer, compare) suggests the close but not verbatim quotation. They may identify persons or places by their vernacular or modern name, refer to other sources corroborating the text or, to the contrary, conveying different information, or simply state that the author is mistaken and give a reference to primary sources or scholarly literature that prove this.

In some series, notes refer to the text "by chapter and verse" or by heading and line number or line number only, by this token avoiding encumbering the original text with little superscript numbers and letters.

---

[9] For generally used abbreviations, see e.g., Antoine Dondaine, "Abréviations latins et signes recommandés pour l'apparat critique des editions des textes médiévaux, *Bulletin de la Société international pour l'étude de la philosophie médiévale* 2 (1960) 142–9.

IV. Indices

Indices should be compiled so that readers interested in such divergent matters as persons, technical terms, or linguistic issues would all easily find reference to their particular subject. It is usual to have at least an "Index personarum" and an "Index geographicus," (or both together in an index of names). An *Index locorum* (of citations), an *Index verborum* (mainly of technical terms, but in a shorter text this can be to all words) that may include spelling variants may be valuable. If the edition is being prepared with a word-processing program, it is easy to generate indices of different sort with relatively little trouble. A subject index (*Index rerum*) is helpful for legal, theoretical and scientific texts, but may be handy for a narrative source as well. It can be straightforward, referring to major subjects (such as "First Crusade") or analytical, grouping the *lemmata* (*lemma* = entry) under a major heading and subheadings (e.g., "Crusade"; subdivided into: sermons on, preparations for, legal character of, etc.). The indices should refer to page and line number or some other unequivocal and close definition of the text, not merely to a page, which, for instance, in a MGH DD in 4° may contain a charter of 600 words or more.

V. Bibliography

Anglo-American publications always, and others usually, have a separate bibliography containing the full title of all works cited in the edition. This is quite useful for researchers working in the same field and also economical, as the complete bibliographical data need not be included in the footnotes, since they can be found in the appendix. Some publishers prefer merely name and short title in the notes and full references in the bibliography.

It is common practice to separate the bibliography into:

(a) manuscript sources with full reference to pressmarks

(b) printed primary sources

(c) secondary literature (books, articles, etc.).

For these matters—just as to the convention for footnotes—editors may have to observe the publisher's house style or some accepted rules (MLA, *Chicago Manual of Style*, etc.).

VI. Maps, Charts, and Illustrations

The inclusion of maps and other illustrations will depend on the character of the text and its problems. They may include facsimiles of the writing of the manuscript cited, the reproduction of one or more passages, for example, colophons, incipits if these are relevant for the decision about the stemma or the filiation. For a chronicle or a travelogue, a map of the region or the places mentioned may be useful, in other cases a table of concordance with earlier (printed) editions may be appropriate.

56 AN INTRODUCTION TO EDITING MANUSCRIPTS

Fig. 5. A German translation of the Bible

Fol. 74r of the so-called Wenceslas Bible, Vienna, ÖNB, Codex Vindobonensis 2760 (c. 1389–1400) [with the kind permission of the Österreichische Nationalbibliothek]

Translating

As knowledge of Latin, Greek, Old Church Slavonic and other "source languages" (such as Old Norse, Anglo-Saxon, Provençal, etc.) has been in decline in recent decades even among medievalists, translations or bi-lingual editions have become ever more widespread and welcome. Moreover, interest in the Middle Ages among non-specialists (or, say, in Latin texts among Slavists), demands that students of medieval texts make their sources available for a wider readership. In fact, it is recommended that an editor should always translate the original text into his/her own language to control how well the edited text sounds, even if not to publish it.

In the following few paragraphs, I summarize the lessons learned from twenty years' of editing the Latin-English bi-lingual series of the Central European Medieval Texts.

To begin with, the best critical edition should be the basis of translation. It may not be necessary to include the complete *apparatus criticus*, as the specialist reader may consult that in the authoritative edition. Still, important variant readings, especially those where the translator is aware of controversial readings, should be noted. For example, in the *Gesta principum Polonorum* of "Gallus Anonymus," the first historically documented ruler, Mieszko, is identified in the best MS Z as *primus nomine vocatus alio*, but the editor (Karol Maleczyński) decided for *prius vocatus nomine alio*. We decided for the translation "the first of that name," considering that is unclear to which "other name" would the author refer. We added a note about the two readings.[1] (Here, again, textual notes

---

[1] *Gesta principum Polonorum. The Deeds of the Princes of the Poles*, Paul W. Knoll and Frank Schaer, trans. with a preface by Thomas Bisson (Buda-

may follow the MGH system of being marked a, b, c). In some cases, especially when the edition is very old, it may be necessary to go back to the "best manuscript," but that is an exception for translations.

TEXT

The translation should aim at a readable, modern presentation of the text, retaining as much of the original rhetoric and style, as possible, without, however, trying to be "archaic." In most translations, an exception are biblical quotations, which are usually given in either the King James Version or the Catholic Douay-Rheims translation. (For medieval texts, the latter would be preferable. True, in CEMT we have abandoned the archaic declension of verbs in that translation.) That translation always implies a certain amount of interpretation, and one should be careful not to go too far in that is a commonplace and needs hardly to be underlined. In case of doubt, one should rather leave unclear matters open and alert the reader to them in a note that may contain hints at different interpretations.

TERMINOLOGY

As translations (and bi-lingual editions) are *per definitionem* aimed at a readership beyond that of specialists, one should be generous with explanatory notes. Besides identifying persons and places (if possible, as usual) and dating events (often in contrast to the text, based on other evidence), the historical context, the local institutions, social groups, offices etc., need more comment that in a scholarly critical edition (usually in footnotes marked 1, 2, 3). The latter often poses problems. The translation of terms specific for medieval government, society, and institutions of a region or country, necessarily different from—in the case of English translation—those of the British Isles is not always easy. This means that an English (or German, French, Spanish, Russian, whatever) word has to be found for those notions that originate in the past of the given

---

pest-New York: Central European University Press, 2003), 62 [CEMT 3].

region but rendered in "international" Latin in the text. Most medieval authors used Latin terms for local features, which they knew from their classical readings, the Vulgate, or other medieval texts. For example, Cosmas of Prague refers to the leading "freemen" (as Lisa Wolverton calls them in her translation) as *comes/comites*.[2] They were certainly neither members of "titled nobility," such as counts, *Grafen* or *comtes*, nor appointed royal officials like Carolingian *comites*. They were probably called *kmet* in the local Slavic vernacular (as similar members of the elite were called *ispán* in medieval Hungary, also translated as *comes* in the sources). It would be certainly misleading to translate the word as "count," unless there is reason to assume (based on the context or other evidence) that the given person is in fact something of a royal officer in charge of some kind of province or city. (For example, in Dalmatia, one can translate Thomas of Split's *comes* as count, probably called locally *conte*).[3]

There are several solutions for this quandary. One may introduce a new term, conspicuously indicating the neologism with a note at the first use—or even discussing this in the Introduction's section on conventions—as Wolverton has done with "freemen." Or, as the editor/translators of the Laws of King St Stephen of Hungary have done with the word *servus* there. Having found problematic the status of persons thus referred (e.g. one was in charge of a castle, not typical for a slave); they used "bondman" (with the appropriate note) and not slave or serf, in order to alert the reader to the problem of interpretation.[4] Another method of overcoming

---

[2] See Cosmas of Prague, *The Chronicle of the Czechs*, trans. Lisa Wolverton (Washington: Catholic University of America Press, 2009).

[3] Thomas of Split, *The History of the Archbishops of Salona and Split, &c.* O. Perić, D. Karbić, Matijević-Sokol, J. R. Sweeney, eds. & trans. (Budapest-New York: CEU Press 2000) [CEMT 4].

[4] *The Laws of the Medieval Kingdom of Hungary/Decreta regni mediaevalis Hungariae*, vol. 1 (1000–1301). J. M. Bak, Gy. Bónis, J. R. Sweeney, eds. & trans., (Idyllwild CA: Schlacks, 1992), 79, nn. 11 and 140. As a matter of fact, we may have been wrong as now Cameron Sutt, *Slavery in Árpád age Hungary* (Leiden: Brill 2005) argues convincingly that in the 11th–12th C. *servi* were personally unfree and bought and sold; the one in charge of the castle being an exception.

this difficulty is to retain in the translation the Latin (or Greek, etc.) term, properly italicized as a foreign word (at least at the first instance) and, again, explain it in a note or the preface. (That is what CEMT editors have done in some volumes with the *comites* in reference to the different medieval elites of the region.) However, too frequent inserts of Latin—or, if known, vernacular—words makes the style heavy or awkward, so one should limit such procedures to the minimum. In the aforementioned legal series, only the vernacular term *ispán* for the Hungarian-Latin *comes* was used.

On the other hand, it is worth exploring to what extent "local" specialties are indeed unique. For example, in the medieval kingdom of Hungary the highest officer of the realm was the *comes palatinus*, his position and privilege more or less "copied" from the medieval Empire. Thus, to translate his office into English as *palatine*, or *count palatine* (and likewise the other court offices of the Master of the Horse, Chief Justice, etc.) may not be inappropriate. True, caution is needed: the term *palatinus* referred in the kingdom of Poland to regional officers, who were not at all similar to the *Pfalzgraf* in Germany or the Hungarian *count palatine* (Hung.: *nádorispán*). Naturally, the translator has to explain all this.

In summary: the problem of terminology has to be faced and explained and this presupposes knowledge of the given society. Thus, sources should be translated by—or in cooperation with—a scholar of the history and society of the region to which the text refers. There have been examples where this was missing and rather silly things came out. The major officer of the Hungarian king's household, the Master of the Doorkeepers (*magister ianitorum*), was in a recent translation (let it remain anonymous) referred to as "master of the janitors," which, in modern (American) English understanding refers to the head of a cleaning company or some kind of custodian.

Personal Names

Another problem is the translation (if at all) of personal names. Our authors, writing in Latin, often translate vernacular names into Latin; Cosmas of Prague calls a man *Deocarus* whose Czech name was clearly Bohumil (Preface to Bk. 2). Both narratives and charters Latinize the vernacular usage of naming a person by his or her father's name: *Johannes filius Pauli* can be translated (as CEMT usage does) as "John son of Paul," but in fact the contemporaries probably called him something like Jan Pawlovicz in Slavic, Johan Pálsson in Scandinavian, or Pálfia János in Hungarian. The name of the martyr saint of Bohemia, Václáv in Czech, is well known through a late successor of his as Wenceslas (the "good king"). It is entirely up to the translator to decide which of the two to use. Václáv may be a bow to modern Czech patriotism; Wenceslas makes the text more familiar to the English reader. There seems to be a trend nowadays in favor of the vernacular; in some publications the first king of Hungary is now called István, a form for which there is no early medieval evidence, even though it is the modern Hungarian version of Stephen/Stephanus. In CEMT we always "Anglicize" names that come from the common Christian calendar (John, Henry, Louis, and so on)—especially in the case of rulers, well known by this name. Otherwise we give vernacular names if known (such as Boleslav or Gyula) or keep the original spelling of the text, if not. However, other choices are possible.

Place Names

Finally, place names. These are a major problem in Central and Eastern Europe (but sometimes in Western Europe as well, see Straßburg vs Strasbourg) where borders and thus the official name of locations and geographical features changed—sometimes more than once—in the course of the centuries. Our principle is to give the present official name (if the place can be unequivocally identified) that can be located on any good atlas—however anachronistic this may sound. Of course, if the city or region has a name in English or whatever other language we translate into, then we use that: Cracow for Kraków, Prague for Praha, etc. If translating into German, one could use Breslau for Wrocław (and many other German names for Central European settlements) but not if into English. It is not easy to decide which of these names are still alive: to call Regensburg *Ratisbon* or Livorno *Leghorn* may be a needless and forced archaism. Considering the frequently present national or ethnic resentment about some modern border and name changes, one should beware that one is treading on dangerous ground. I lost a "patriotic" Hungarian collaborator who would not agree to write Košice for the now Slovak town of Kassa/Kaschau that was for centuries part of the kingdom of Hungary.

If there is a significant number of place names that have several forms, the best solution is to add a Gazetteer to the end of the volume, in which the Latin (or whatever else) of the text, the form used in the translation and any other forms (historical or modern) are tabulated.

Considering all these problems, in the Introduction to a translation (or bi-lingual edition) the chapter on the "present edition" has to be expanded in order to clarify the editor/translator's choice of conventions regarding terminology, and names of persons and places. This is the place to explain why, for example, *comes* was left in the Latin form and *Alba Bulgarorum* is given as Belgrade.

***

"And now"—in the words of Professor Huygens—"if you are not discouraged by the fact that all the above represents no more than a sketch of a long and arduous process"[5] go ahead, brush up on your classics, your Church Fathers and the Bible, and risk editing or translating a medieval manuscript. Or, at least be able expertly to criticize or improve the edition/translation of others.

---

[5] Huygens, *Ars edendi*, 72.

BIBLIOGRAPHY

Agati, Maria Luisa, *The Manuscript. From East to West: For a Comparative Codicology* (Rome: "L'Erma" di Bretschneider, 2016).

Ailred of Rievaulx, *Quand Jesus eut Douze Ans,* ed. Anselme Hoste (Paris: Cerf, 1987). [Sources Chrétiennes 60].

Anonymi Bele regis notarii Gesta Hungarorum/Anonymus, notary of King Béla, The Deeds of the Hungarians, ed. and trans. Marty Rady and László Veszprémy, in: *Anonymus and Master Roger* 2–129 (Budapest-New York: Central European University Press, 2010) [CEMT 5].

ARTFL Project, https://www.lib.uchicago.edu/efts/ARTFL/public/bibles/vulgate.search.html

Bak, J. M., Gy. Bónis, J. R. Sweeney, eds. & trans., *The Laws of the Medieval Kingdom of Hungary/Decreta regni mediaevalis Hungariae*, vol. 1 (1000–1301). (Idyllwild CA: Schlacks, ed. 2 rev., 1999).

Bausi, Alessandro, gen.ed. *Comparative Oriental Manuscript Studies: An Introduction*, (Hamburg: Tredition, 2015), also: http://www1.uni-hamburg.de/COMST/handbookonline.html.

Bedae Venerabilis Historia ecclesiastica gentis Anglorum, ed. Carolus Plummer, 2 vols. (Oxford: Clarendon Press 1896; repr. several times).

Bédier, Joseph, "La tradition manuscrite du *Lais del'ombre*. Reflexions sur l'art d'éditer les anciens textes" *Romania* 54 (1928) 161–96, 321–56.

Bell, M. ed., "Life of St. Wulfric of Haselbury", *Sommerset Record Society* 47 (1933).

Bévenot, Maurice, *The tradition of manuscripts: a study in the transmission of St. Cyprian's treatises*, (Oxford: The Clarendon Press, 1961).

Bibliotheca Corviniana Online, http://jekely.blogspot.hu/p/bibliotheca-corviniana.html.

Bischoff, Bernhard, Latin Palaeography: Antiquity and the Middle Ages (Cambridge: CUP, 1999).

Boyle, Leonard E., *Medieval Latin Paleography: A Bibliographical Orientation* (Toronto: Toronto Medieval Bibliographies, 1984).

———, "Optimist and Recensionist: 'Common Errors' and 'Common Variants'?" in: *Latin Script and Letters A.D. 400–900. Feschschrift Presented to Ludwig Bieler on the Occasion of His 70th Birthday*, John O'Meara and Berndt Neumann, eds. 264–74 (Leiden: Brill, 1976).

Briquet, C. M., *Les filigranes*, (Paris: Picard, 1907; repr. 1968, ed. A. Stevenson).

Burchardi Ursbergensi Chronicon, eds. Oswald Holder-Egger and Bernhard von Simson. (Hanover: Hahn 1916) [MGH SS rer. Germ. in us. schol. 16.]

Cárcel Ortí, Maria Milagros, ed. *Vocabulaire Internationale de Diplomatique* (ed. 2, Valencia: Collecció Oberta, 1997)

Carruthers, Mary, *The Book of Memory. A Study of Memory in Medieval Culture* (Cambridge: CUP, 1990).

Castellani, A., *Bédier avait-il raison? Le methode de Lachmann dans les éditions des textes du moyen âge*, (Fribourg: Presses Univ., 1957).

Chibnall, Marjorie, trans., *The Ecclesiastical History of Orderic Vitalis*, 6 vols. (Oxford: Oxford University Press, 1968–1980).

Clemens, Raymond and Timothy Graham, *Introduction to Manuscript Studies* (Ithaca, N.Y.: Cornell University Press, 2007).

Clement, Richard, "Medieval Book Production", http://works.bepress.com/Richard_clement/3.

Clementíne Vulgate Project, http://vulsearch.sourceforge.net/cgi-bin/vulsearch.

Colophons de manuscrits occidentaux des origins au XV^{Ie} siècle, 6 vols. (Fribourg: Éditions universitaires, 1965–82).

Compagni, Dino, *Cronica delle cose correnti ne' tempi suoi*, ed. Ludovico Antonio Muratori, Rerum Italicarum scriptores 9: 467–536 (Milan, 1726).

Cosmas of Prague, *Chronica Bohemorum. The Chronicle of the Czechs*, eds. J. M. Bak and P. Rychterová, tr. P. Mutlová and M. Rady, annot. Jan Hasil *et al.* (Budapest-New York: CEU Press, 2017) [CEMT].

———, *The Chronicle of the Czechs*, trans. Lisa Wolverton (Washington: Catholic University of America Press, 2009).

Croix Bouton, J.de la, ed., *Les plus anciens textes de Cîteaux*, (Achel: Abbaye cistercinne, 1974) [Commentarii Cistercienses Studia et Documenta 2].

Csapodi, Csaba, *Bibliotheca Corviniana: The library of King Matthias Corvinus of Hungary*, (Budapest: Corvina, 1981).

Davis, Charles T., "The Malispini Question," *Studi Medievali* ser. 3, 10 (1969) 215–54 .

Delaissé, Leon M. J., *Le Manuscrit autographe de Thomas Kempis et "L'Imitation de Jésus Christ". Examen archéologique et édition diplomatique du Bruxellensis 5855-61*, (Paris–Brussels: Erasme, 1956).

Dino Compagni's Chronicle of Florence, tr. and ed. D. E. Bronstein, (Philadelphia: Penn. U. Press, 1986).

Dondaine, Antoine, "Abréviations latins et signes recommandés pour l'apparat critique des editions des textes médiévaux, *Bulletin de la Société international pour l'étude de la philosophie médiévale* 2 (1960) 142–9.

Dunphy, Graeme, gen.ed., *The Encyclopedia of the Medieval Chronicle* 2 vols. (Leiden: Brill 2010).

Eder, Maciej, "In search of the author of Chronica Polonorum ascribed to Gallus Anonymus: A stylometric reconnaissance", *Acta Poloniae Historica* 112 (2015) 5–23. (Available online as http://www.aph-ihpan.edu.pl/images/112_01_Eder.pdf).

Eklund, Sven, "The use and abuse of cursus in textual criticism," documents.irevues.inist.fr/bitstream/handle/2042/3361/02%20TEXTE.pdf.

Fälschungen im Mittelalter 6 vols. (Hanover: Hahn, 1988) [MGH Schriften 33: 1-6].

Five millennium catalog of solar eclipses, http://eclipse.gsfc.nasa.gov/SEcat5/SEcatalog.html

Galbraith, Vivian Hunter, "An Autograph MS of Ranulph Hidgen's Polychronicon" *Huntington Library Quarterly* 23 (1959/60) 1–18.

Gesta principum Polonorum. The Deeds of the Princes of the Poles, trans. Paul W. Knoll and Frank Schaer, with a preface by Thomas Bisson (Budapest-New York: Central European University Press, 2003) [CEMT 3].

Hall, F. W., A *Companion to Classical Texts* (Oxford: The Clarendon Press, 1913.)

Henrici Chronicon Livoniae, eds. Leonid Arbusow and Albertus Bauer (Hanover: Hahn, 1955) [MGH SS. rer. Germ. in us. schol. 31].

Hildegardis Bingensis Epistolarium, Pars I, ed. L. Van Acker, (Turnholt: Brepols, 1991) [Corpus Christianorum Continuatio Mediaevalis 91].

Huygens, R. B. C., *Ars edendi* (Turholt: Brepols, 2000).

———, "Looking for Manuscripts ... and Then?" http://www.illinoismedieval.org/ems/VOL4/huygens.html.

In Principio. Incipit index of Latin texts, http://www.brepolis.net/pdf/Brepolis_INPR_EN.pdf

Ker, Neil Ripley, *Medieval Libraries of Great Britain: A list of surviving books*, ed. 2 (London: Royal Hist. Soc. 1964).

———, *Medieval Manuscripts in British Libraries* (Oxford: The Clarendon Press, 1969.

Kristeller, Paul Oskar, *Latin Manuscript Books Before 1600: A List of the Printed Catalogues and Unpublished Inventories of Extant Collections*, 4th. Rev. ed. S. Krämer (Munich: MGH, 1993), [MGH Hilfmittel 13].

Latin Vulgate, http://www.latinvulgate.com.

Lehmann, Paul, *Erforschung des Mittelalters* 5 vols., (Stuttgart: Heinemann, 1959-1962).

Library of Latin Texts A and B, http://www.brepolis.net/pdf/Brepolis_LLT_EN.pdf.

Likhachev, N. P., *Paleograficheskoe znachanie bumazhnykh znakon*, (St. Petersburg, 1899).

Likhachev's watermarks: An English language version, eds. J. S. G. Simmons and Bé van Ginneken-van de Kasteele, (Amsterdam: Paper Publication Society, 1994), 2 vols.

Love, Harold, *Attributing Authorship: An Introduction* (Cambridge: CUP, 2002).

Lungo, Isidoro del, *Dino Compagni e sua cronica*, 4 vols. (Florence: Le Monnier 1879-87; e-book ed. 2015).

Magistri Adam Bremensis Gesta Hammaburgensis ecclesiae pontificorum, ed. M. Schmeidler, (ed. 3, Hanover: Hahn 1917) [MGH SS rer. Germ. in us. sch. 2].

Mantello, F.A.C. and A. G. Rigg, eds. *Medieval Latin: An Introduction and Bibliographical Guide*, (Washington, D.C.: The Catholic University of America Press, 1996).

Medievalfragments, https://medievalfragments.wordpress.com/2012/09/28/give-me-a-drink-scribal-colophons-in-medieval-manuscripts/.

Migne. Jacques Paul, *Patrologiae Cursus Completus. Series Latina* (Paris 1841–55).

Monastic Manuscript Project, http://www.earlymedievalmonasticism.org/Catalogues-of-Latin-Manuscripts.html.

Norbert, Dag, *Manuel pratique de latin médiéval* (Paris: Picard, 1980). English trans. by R. H. Johnson, http://www.orbilat.com/Languages/Latin_Medieval/Dag_Norberg/index.html.

Ottonis et Rahewini Gesta Frederici imperatoris I, ed. Georg Waitz (ed. 3, Hanover: Hahn, 1912) [MGH SS rer. Germ. in us. schol. 46].

Parkes, M. B., *Pause and Effect: An Introduction to the History of Punctuation in the West* (Farnham: Ashgate 1992).

Philippi, Friedrich, "Norberts Vita Bennonis eine Fälschung?" *Neues Archiv*, 25 (1900), 767–96.

Powicke, F. M., ed., *The Life of Ailred of Rievaulx by Walter Daniel* (London: Nelson, 1950.)

Prestwich, John O., "King Aethelhere and the Battle of the Winwaed" *English Historical Review*, 83 (1968), 89–95.

Quirin, Heinz, *Einführung in das Studium der mittelalterlichen Geschichte* (5th ed. Stuttgart: Steiner, 1991).

Raabe, Wesley, *Collation in scholarly editing: An Introduction* https://wraabe.wordpress.com/2008/07/26/collation-in-scholarly-editing-an-introduction-draft/.

Reynolds, L.D. and G. Wilson, *Scribes and Scholars: A Guide to the Transmission of Greek and Latin Literature*, (2d ed., Oxford: Clarendon Press, 1974).

Rogerius of Oradea, "Epistle on the Sorrowful Lament upon the Destruction of Hungary by the Tatars" by Master Roger, tr. J. M. Bak and Martyn Rady in: *Anonymus and Master Roger*, 132–228 (Budapest: CEU Press 2010) [CEMT 5]

Rychterová, Pavlina, "The Manuscripts of Grünberg and Königinhof: Romantic Lies about the Glorious Past of the Czech Nation" in: *Manufacturing a Past for the Present: Authenticity and Forgery in Nineteenth Century Texts and Objects*, J. M. Bak, G. Klaniczay, P. Geary, eds. 3–30 (Leiden: Brill, 2015).

Scheffer-Boichorst, Paul, "Die florentinische Geschichte der Malaspini eine Fälschung, "*Historische Zeitschrift* 24 (1870) 274–313.

———, "Norbert's Vita Bennonis Osnabrugensis episcopi eine Fälschung?"*Sitzungberichte der kgl. Preussischen Akademie der Wissenschaften in Berlin*, 1901, 132–68.

Schmale, Franz-Josef, "Fälschungen in der Geschichtsschreibung," in: *Fälschungen* 1: 121–32.

Southern, R. W., ed. and trans., *The life of St Anselm, archbishop of Canterbury* (2nd ed., Oxford: Oxford University Press, 1972).

Spiegel, Gabrielle M., *The past as text: Theory and practice of medieval historiography* (Baltimore: Johns Hopkins University Press, 1997).

Stamatatos, Efstathios, '"A Survey of Modern Authorship Attribution Methods", *Journal of the American Society for Information Science and Technology*, 60 (2009), 538–56.

Strecker, Karl, ed. *Die lateinischen Dichter des deutschen Mittelalters*, (Leipzig: Hiersemann, 1937) [MGH Poet. 5.1].

Studi e testi 318, Bibliogrfia dei fondi manoscritti della Bibliotheca Vaticana (Rome: Bibliotheca Apostolica Vaticana 1986)

Sutt, Cameron, *Slavery in Árpád age Hungary* (Leiden: Brill 2005).

Thomas of Split, *The History of the Archbishops of Salona and Split, &c.* O. Perić, D. Karbić, Matijević-Sokol, J. R. Sweeney, eds. & trans. (Budapest-New York: CEU Press 2000) [CEMT 4].

Thurocz, Johannes de, *Chronica Hungarorum*, I. *Textus*, eds. Elisabeth Galántai, Julius Kristó (Budapest: Akadémiai Kiadó, 1985); II. *Commentarii* 2 vols. eds. Elemér Mályusz, Julius Kristó, (ibid. 1988) [Bibliotheca Scriptorum Medii Recentisque Aevorum, S.N. 7–9].

Tillotson, Diana, *Medieval writing*, http://medievalwriting.50megs.com/whatis.htm.

Timpanaro, Sebastiano, *The Genesis of Lachmann's Method* (Chicago and London: University of Chicago Press, 2005).

Tolochko, Oleksyi, "On 'Nestor the Chronicler'", *Harvard Ukrainian Studies* 29 (2007) 1–31.

Vita Bennonis episcopi Osnabrugiensis auctore Norberto abbate Iburgensi, ed. Harry Bresslau (Hanover: Hahn, 1902) [MGH SS rer. Germ. in us. schol. 56].

Wasserzeichen des Mittelalters Projekt, www.wzma.at.

West, Martin L., *Textual Criticism and Editorial Technique applicable to Greek and Latin texts*, (Stuttgart: Teubner, 1973).

Western Illuminated Manuscripts: A Catalogue of the Collection in Cambridge University Library by Paul Binski and Patrick Zutshi, with the collaboration of Stella Panayotova (Cambridge, 2011).

William of Malmesbury, *De Antiquitate Glastoniensis Ecclesiae*, ed. and trans. J. Scott (Woodbridge: Boydell, 1991).

Wolverton, Lisa, *Cosmas of Prague: Narrative, classicism, politics* (Washington D.C.: The Catholic University of America Press, 2015).